2

AN INQUIRY EARTH SCIENCE PROGRAM

INVESTIGATING OUR DYNAMIC PLANET

Michael J. Smith Ph.D.
American Geological Institute

John B. Southard Ph.D.
Massachusetts Institute of Technology

Colin Mably
Curriculum Developer

Developed by the American Geological Institute
Supported by the National Science Foundation and
the American Geological Institute Foundation

Published by
It's About Time Inc., Armonk, NY

It's About Time, Inc.
84 Business Park Drive, Armonk, NY 10504
Phone (914) 273-2233 Fax (914) 273-2227
Toll Free (888) 698-TIME
www.Its-About-Time.com

Publisher
Laurie Kreindler

Project Editor
Ruta Demery

Design
John Nordland

Production Manager
Joan Lee

Associate Editor
Al Mari

Creative Artwork
Dennis Falcon

Safety Reviewer
Dr. Edward Robeck

Production
Burmar Technical Corporation

Technical Art
Armstrong/Burmar

Senior Photo Consultant
Bruce F. Molnia

Photo Research
Caitlin Callahan

Contributing Writers
William Jones
Matthew Smith

Illustrations and Photos
P5, P13, P15, P18, P19, P20, P23, P24, P25, P27, P28, P31, P33, P36, P37, P38, P39, P43 (map), P45 (map), P52, P54 (source: Edwin Colbert, "Wandering Lands and Animals." Dover Publishers, 1985), P55 (map), P57, P58, P67, illustrations by Stuart Armstrong; P41, Eric Bergmanis; P8, technical art by Burmar Technical Corporation; P22, Bob Christman; Pxi (lower left), Digital Vision Royalty Free Images: North America; P30, Perle Dorr; Pxii, P2, P9, P11, P33, P43, P53, P63, illustrations by Dennis Falcon; P4, courtesy of Fisher Science Education Co.; P61, Jim D. Griggs, U.S. Geological Survey Hawaiian Volcano Observatory; P68, Roger Hutchison; Pxi (top left), Pxii, P51, Martin Miller; P1, courtesy of the Paleontological Research Institute; P6, PhotoDisc; P37, John Shelton; P46, P66, J.K. Nakata; Pxi (upper right), H.G. Wilshire: from the "The October 17, 1989, Loma Prieta, California, Earthquake – Selected Photographs," U.S. Geological Survey; P49, Barbara Zahm

All student activities in this textbook have been designed to be as safe as possible, and have been reviewed by professionals specifically for that purpose. As well, appropriate warnings concerning potential safety hazards are included where applicable to particular activities. However, responsibility for safety remains with the student, the classroom teacher, the school principals, and the school board.

Printed and bound in the United States of America

ISBN #1-58591-081-3

1 2 3 4 5 QC 06 05 04 03 02

This project was supported, in part, by the
National Science Foundation (grant no. 9353035)

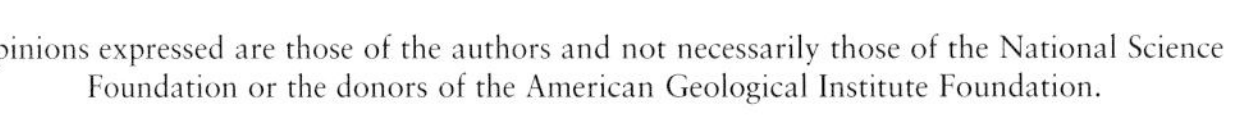

Opinions expressed are those of the authors and not necessarily those of the National Science Foundation or the donors of the American Geological Institute Foundation.

Acknowledgements

Principal Investigator

Michael Smith is Director of Education at the American Geological Institute in Alexandria, Virginia. Dr. Smith worked as an exploration geologist and hydrogeologist. He began his Earth Science teaching career with Shady Side Academy in Pittsburgh, PA in 1988 and most recently taught Earth Science at the Charter School of Wilmington, DE. He earned a doctorate from the University of Pittsburgh's Cognitive Studies in Education Program and joined the faculty of the University of Delaware School of Education in 1995. Dr. Smith received the Outstanding Earth Science Teacher Award for Pennsylvania from the National Association of Geoscience Teachers in 1991, served as Secretary of the National Earth Science Teachers Association, and is a reviewer for Science Education and The Journal of Research in Science Teaching. He worked on the Delaware Teacher Standards, Delaware Science Assessment, National Board of Teacher Certification, and AAAS Project 2061 Curriculum Evaluation programs.

Senior Writer

John Southard received his undergraduate degree from the Massachusetts Institute of Technology in 1960 and his doctorate in geology from Harvard University in 1966. After a National Science Foundation postdoctoral fellowship at the California Institute of Technology, he joined the faculty at the Massachusetts Institute of Technology, where he is currently Professor of Geology. He was awarded the MIT School of Science teaching prize in 1989 and was one of the first cohorts of first MacVicar Fellows at MIT, in recognition of excellence in undergraduate teaching. He has taught numerous undergraduate courses in introductory geology, sedimentary geology, field geology, and environmental Earth science both at MIT and in Harvard's adult education program. He was editor of the Journal of Sedimentary Petrology from 1992 to 1996, and he continues to do technical editing of scientific books and papers for SEPM, a professional society for sedimentary geology. Dr. Southard received the 2001 Neil Miner Award from the National Association of Geoscience Teachers.

Project Director/Curriculum Designer

Colin Mably has been a key curriculum developer for several NSF-supported national curriculum projects. As learning materials designer to the American Geological Institute, he has directed the design and development of the IES curriculum modules and also training workshops for pilot and field-test teachers.

Project Team

Marcus Milling
Executive Director - AGI, VA

Michael Smith
Principal Investigator - Director of Education - AGI, VA

Colin Mably
Project Director/Curriculum Designer - Educational Visions, MD

Matthew Smith
Project Coordinator
Program Manager - AGI, VA

Fred Finley
Project Evaluator
University of Minnesota, MN

Joe Moran
American Meteorological Society

Lynn Lindow
Pilot Test Evaluator
University of Minnesota, MN

Harvey Rosenbaum
Field Test Evaluator
Montgomery School District, MD

Ann Benbow
Project Advisor - American Chemical Society, DC

Robert Ridky
Original Project Director
University of Maryland, MD

Chip Groat
Original Principal Investigator - University of Texas
El Paso, TX

Marilyn Suiter
Original Co-principal Investigator - AGI, VA

William Houston
Field Test Manager

Caitlin Callahan - Project Assistant

Original and Contributing Authors

Oceans
George Dawson
Florida State University, FL

Joseph F. Donoghue
Florida State University, FL

Ann Benbow
American Chemical Society

Michael Smith
American Geological Institute

Soil
Robert Ridky
University of Maryland, MD

Colin Mably - LaPlata, MD

John Southard
Massachusetts Institute of Technology, MA

Michael Smith
American Geological Institute

Fossils
Robert Gastaldo
Colby College, ME

Colin Mably - LaPlata, MD

Michael Smith
American Geological Institute

Climate and Weather
Mike Mogil
How the Weather Works, MD

Ann Benbow
American Chemical Society

Joe Moran
American Meteorological Society

Michael Smith
American Geological Institute

Energy Resources
Laurie Martin-Vermilyea
American Geological Institute

Michael Smith
American Geological Institute

Dynamic Planet
Michael Smith
American Geological Institute

Rocks and Landforms
Michael Smith
American Geological Institute

Water as a Resource
Ann Benbow
American Chemical Society

Michael Smith
American Geological Institute

Materials and Minerals
Mary Poulton
University of Arizona, AZ

Colin Mably - LaPlata, MD

Michael Smith
American Geological Institute

Advisory Board

Jane Crowder
Middle School Teacher, WA

Kerry Davidson
Louisiana Board of Regents, LA

Joseph D. Exline
Educational Consultant, VA

Louis A. Fernandez
California State University, CA

Frank Watt Ireton
National Earth Science Teachers Association, DC

LeRoy Lee
Wisconsin Academy of Sciences, Arts and Letters, WI

Donald W. Lewis
Chevron Corporation, CA

James V. O'Connor (deceased)
University of the District of Columbia, DC

Roger A. Pielke Sr.
Colorado State University, CO

Dorothy Stout
Cypress College, CA

Lois Veath
Advisory Board Chairperson
Chadron State College, NE

Pilot Test Teachers

Debbie Bambino
Philadelphia, PA

Barbara Barden - Rittman, OH

Louisa Bliss - Bethlehem, NH

Mike Bradshaw - Houston TX

Greta Branch - Reno, NV

Garnetta Chain - Piscataway, NJ

Roy Chambers Portland, OR

Laurie Corbett - Sayre, PA

James Cole - New York, NY

Collette Craig - Reno, NV

Anne Douglas - Houston, TX

Jacqueline Dubin - Roslyn, PA

Jane Evans - Media, PA

Gail Gant - Houston, TX

Joan Gentry - Houston, TX

Pat Gram - Aurora, OH

Robert Haffner - Akron, OH

Joe Hampel - Swarthmore, PA

Wayne Hayes - West Green, GA

Mark Johnson - Reno, NV

Cheryl Joloza - Philadelphia, PA

Jeff Luckey - Houston, TX

Karen Luniewski
Reistertown, MD

Cassie Major - Plainfield, VT

Carol Miller - Houston, TX

Melissa Murray - Reno, NV

Mary-Lou Northrop
North Kingstown, RI

Keith Olive - Ellensburg, WA

Tracey Oliver - Philadelphia, PA

Nicole Pfister - Londonderry, VT

Beth Price - Reno, NV

Joyce Ramig - Houston, TX

Julie Revilla - Woodbridge, VA

Steve Roberts - Meredith, NH

Cheryl Skipworth
Philadelphia, PA

Brent Stenson - Valdosta, GA

Elva Stout - Evans, GA

Regina Toscani
Philadelphia, PA

Bill Waterhouse
North Woodstock, NH

Leonard White
Philadelphia, PA

Paul Williams - Lowerford, VT

Bob Zafran - San Jose, CA

Missi Zender - Twinsburg, OH

Field Test Teachers

Eric Anderson - Carson City, NV

Katie Bauer - Rockport, ME

Kathleen Berdel - Philadelphia, PA

Wanda Blake - Macon, GA

Beverly Bowers
Mannington, WV

Rick Chiera - Monroe Falls, OH

Don Cole - Akron, OH

Patte Cotner - Bossier City, LA

Johnny DeFreese - Haughton, LA

Mary Devine - Astoria, NY

Cheryl Dodes - Queens, NY

Brenda Engstrom - Warwick, RI

Lisa Gioe-Cordi - Brooklyn, NY

Pat Gram - Aurora, OH

Mark Johnson - Reno, NV

Chicory Koren - Kent, OH

Marilyn Krupnick
Philadelphia, PA

Melissa Loftin - Bossier City, LA

Janet Lundy - Reno, NV

Vaughn Martin - Easton, ME

Anita Mathis - Fort Valley, GA

Laurie Newton - Truckee, NV

Debbie O'Gorman - Reno, NV

Joe Parlier - Barnesville, GA

Sunny Posey - Bossier City, LA

Beth Price - Reno, NV

Stan Robinson
Mannington, WV

Mandy Thorne
Mannington, WV

Marti Tomko
Westminster, MD

Jim Trogden - Rittman, OH

Torri Weed - Stonington, ME

Gene Winegart - Shreveport, LA

Dawn Wise - Peru, ME

Paula Wright - Gray, GA

IMPORTANT NOTICE

The *Investigating Earth Systems*™ series of modules is intended for use by students under the direct supervision of a qualified teacher. The experiments described in this book involve substances that may be harmful if they are misused or if the procedures described are not followed. Read cautions carefully and follow all directions. Do not use or combine any substances or materials not specifically called for in carrying out experiments. Other substances are mentioned for educational purposes only and should not be used by students unless the instructions specifically indicate.

The materials, safety information, and procedures contained in this book are believed to be reliable. This information and these procedures should serve only as a starting point for classroom or laboratory practices, and they do not purport to specify minimal legal standards or to represent the policy of the American Geological Institute. No warranty, guarantee, or representation is made by the American Geological Institute as to the accuracy or specificity of the information contained herein, and the American Geological Institute assumes no responsibility in connection therewith. The added safety information is intended to provide basic guidelines for safe practices. It cannot be assumed that all necessary warnings and precautionary measures are contained in the printed material and that other additional information and measures may not be required.

This work is based upon work supported by the National Science Foundation under Grant No. 9353035 with additional support from the Chevron Corporation. Any opinions, findings, and conclusions or recommendations expressed in this publication are those of the authors and do not necessarily reflect the views of the National Science Foundation or the Chevron Corporation. Any mention of trade names does not imply endorsement from the National Science Foundation or the Chevron Corporation.

Table of Contents

Using Investigating Earth Systems

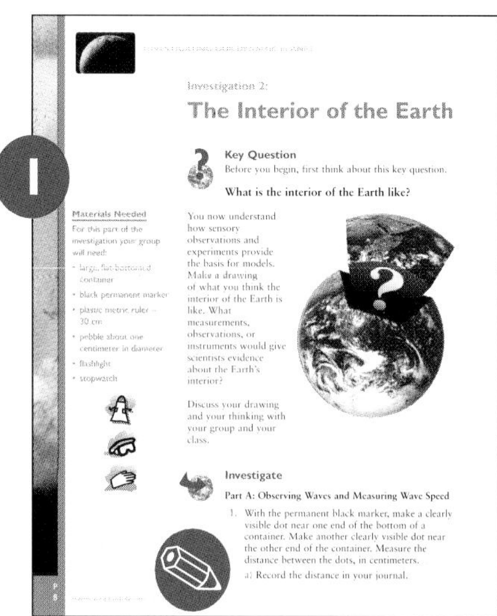

1

Investigation 2:

The Interior of the Earth

Key Question

Before you begin, first think about this key question.

What is the interior of the Earth like?

Materials Needed

For this part of the investigation your group will need:

- large, flat-bottomed container
- black permanent marker
- plastic metric ruler – 30 cm
- pebble about one centimeter in diameter
- flashlight
- stopwatch

You now understand how sensory observations and experiments provide the basis for models. Make a drawing of what you think the interior of the Earth is like. What measurements, observations, or instruments would give scientists evidence about the Earth's interior?

Discuss your drawing and your thinking with your group and your class.

Investigate

Part A: Observing Waves and Measuring Wave Speed

1. With the permanent black marker, make a clearly visible dot near one end of the bottom of a container. Make another clearly visible dot near the other end of the container. Measure the distance between the dots, in centimeters.
   a) Record the distance in your journal.

P 8

2

2. Pour water into the container to a depth of 2 to 3 cm. Let the water come to rest, until the water surface is mirror smooth.
3. Have one student hold a pebble 5 cm over one of the marks on the bottom of the container.
4. Have a second student shine a flashlight beam straight down on the other mark. This student should lean directly over the flashlight to see the reflection of the beam from the water surface. This student should also hold a stopwatch and be familiar with how it works.
5. While the second student stares carefully at the reflection of the flashlight beam, the first student drops the pebble into the water. The second student starts the stopwatch when he or she hears the pebble enter the water. The second student stops the watch when he or she first detects motion of the water in the flashlight beam. This motion signals the arrival of the wave.
   a) Record the time on the stopwatch as the travel time of the wave.

Inquiry

Conducting an Investigation

After scientists have designed an investigation, they conduct their test. The test must be free from uncontrolled variables. In this case you must be sure that the pebble is dropped from the same height each time, and the stopwatch is started and stopped at the correct time. Tests are often repeated several times to ensure reliable and valid results.

Wear goggles when dropping the pebble. Wash your hands after the activity.

3

Place two pieces of cardboard so they touch, side by side, on top of the syrup in the center of the container.

2. Before you light the candle, predict what you think will happen to the cardboard as the corn syrup heats up.
   a) Record your prediction, and also the reason(s) for your prediction.
3. When you have had your equipment CHECKED FOR SAFETY, light the candle and slide it under the center of the container.
   a) While waiting for the corn syrup to heat, draw a side view of the pan alongside your prediction and reason(s).
4. Watch carefully as the corn syrup heats up.
   a) Record your observations and interpretations in your journal.
   b) On your "side-view" drawing of the experimental setup, show any movement of the cardboard with solid arrows.
   c) Show the movement of the corn syrup with dashed arrows.
5. Next you will watch a demonstration.

   A clear, heat-proof beaker, two-thirds full with water is placed on a hot plate.

   When the water is simmering (not boiling), one cup of oatmeal will be poured into the beaker. One drop of food coloring will be added. Finally, some sawdust will be added.

Inquiry

Making Diagrams

Sometimes the best way to show the results of a scientific investigation is by drawing a diagram. Complicated concepts can often be illustrated more easily than they can be explained in words. The diagram should be labeled and described in a sentence or two.

Be careful with open flames. Tie back hair and push back or roll up loose clothing. Remove loose jewelry from near your hands. Wear goggles. Allow the syrup to cool completely before touching the heat-resistant container. Clean up spills immediately.

This is a demonstration only. Once the oatmeal is taken into the lab, it must be considered contaminated because it is used in a science activity. Do not consume the oatmeal.

P 23

Look for the following features in this module to help you learn about the Earth system.

1. Key Question

Before you begin, you will be asked to think about the key question you will investigate. You do not need to come up with a correct answer. Instead you will be expected to take some time to think about what you already know. You can then share your ideas with your small group and with the class.

2. Investigate

Geoscientists learn about the Earth system by doing investigations. That is exactly what you will be doing. Sometimes you will be given the procedures to follow. Other times you will need to decide what question you want to investigate and what procedure to follow.

3. Inquiry

You will use inquiry processes to investigate and solve problems in an orderly way. Look for these reminders about the processes you are using.

Throughout your investigations you will keep your own journal. Your journal is like one that scientists keep when they investigate a scientific question. You can enter anything you think is important during the investigation. There will also be questions after many of the **Investigate** steps for you to answer and enter in your journal. You will also need to think about how the Earth works as a set of systems. You can write the connections you make after each investigation on your *Earth System Connection* sheet in your journal.

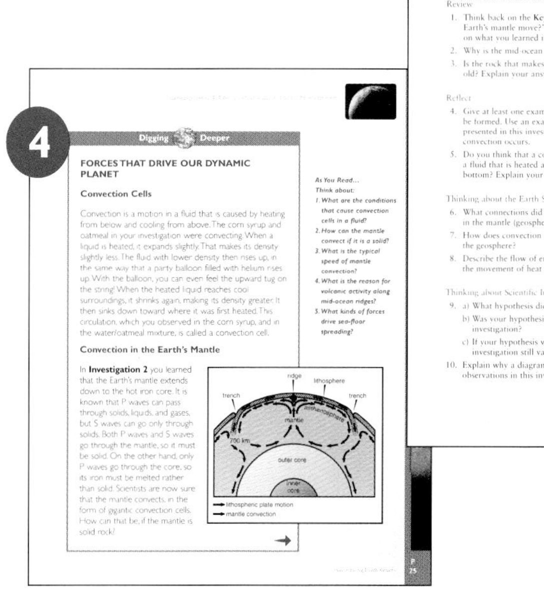

4

Digging Deeper

FORCES THAT DRIVE OUR DYNAMIC PLANET

Convection Cells

Convection is a motion in a fluid that is caused by heating from below and cooling from above. The corn syrup and oatmeal in your investigation were convecting. When a liquid is heated, it expands slightly. That makes its density slightly less. The fluid with lower density then rises up, in the same way that a party balloon filled with helium rises up. With the balloon, you can even feel the upward tug on the string! When the heated liquid reaches cool surroundings, it shrinks again, making its density greater. It then sinks down toward where it was first heated. This circulation, which you observed in the corn syrup, and in the water/oatmeal mixture, is called a convection cell.

Convection in the Earth's Mantle

In **Investigation 2** you learned that the Earth's mantle extends down to the hot iron core. It is known that P waves can pass through solids, liquids, and gases, but S waves can go only through solids. Both P waves and S waves go through the mantle, so it must be solid. On the other hand, only P waves go through the core, so its iron must be melted rather than solid. Scientists are now sure that the mantle convects, in the form of gigantic convection cells. How can that be, if the mantle is solid rock?

As You Read...
Think about:
1. What are the conditions that cause convection cells in a fluid?
2. How can the mantle convect if it is a solid?
3. What is the typical speed of mantle convection?
4. What is the reason for volcanic activity along mid-ocean ridges?
5. What kinds of forces drive sea-floor spreading?

P
25

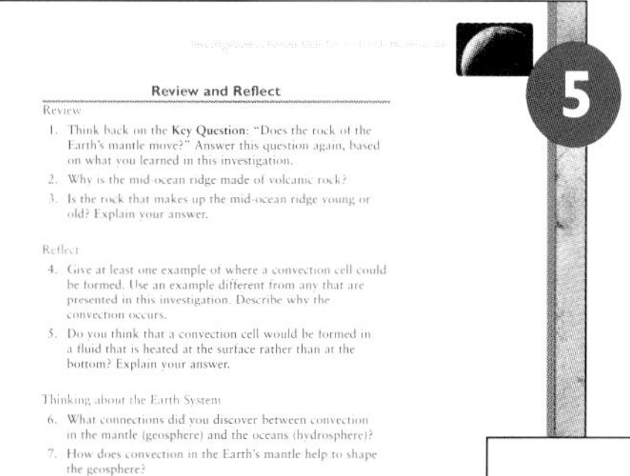

5

Review and Reflect

Review

1. Think back on the **Key Question**: "Does the rock of the Earth's mantle move?" Answer this question again, based on what you learned in this investigation.
2. Why is the mid-ocean ridge made of volcanic rock?
3. Is the rock that makes up the mid-ocean ridge young or old? Explain your answer.

Reflect

4. Give at least one example of where a convection cell could be formed. Use an example different from any that are presented in this investigation. Describe why the convection occurs.
5. Do you think that a convection cell would be formed in a fluid that is heated at the surface rather than at the bottom? Explain your answer.

Thinking about the Earth System

6. What connections did you discover between convection in the mantle (geosphere) and the oceans (hydrosphere)?
7. How does convection in the Earth's mantle help to shape the geosphere?
8. Describe the flow of energy in the geosphere. Think about the movement of heat energy during mantle convection.

Thinking about Scientific Inquiry

9. a) What hypothesis did you form in this investigation?
b) Was your hypothesis proven right or wrong by your investigation?
c) If your hypothesis was wrong, are the results of the investigation still valid? Explain.
10. Explain why a diagram was a good way to show your observations in this investigation.

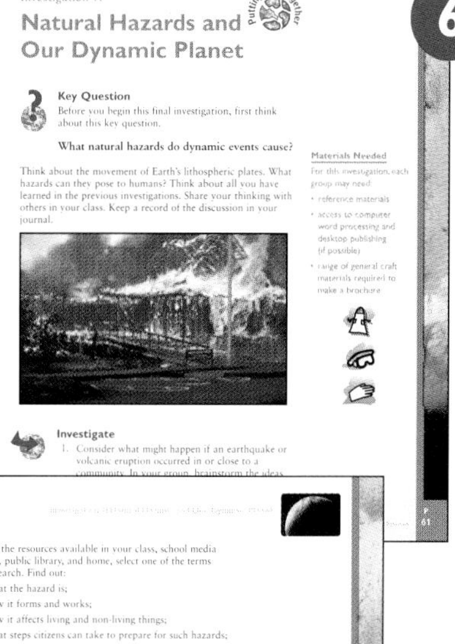

6

Investigation 7:

Natural Hazards and Our Dynamic Planet

Putting It All Together

Key Question

Before you begin this final investigation, first think about this key question.

What natural hazards do dynamic events cause?

Think about the movement of Earth's lithospheric plates. What hazards can they pose to humans? Think about all you have learned in the previous investigations. Share your thinking with others in your class. Keep a record of the discussion in your journal.

Materials Needed

For this investigation, each group may need:
- reference materials
- access to computer word processing and desktop publishing (if possible)
- range of general craft materials required to make a brochure

Investigate

1. Consider what might happen if an earthquake or volcanic eruption occurred in or close to a community. In your group, brainstorm the ideas...

P
61

4. Using the resources available in your class, school media center, public library, and home, select one of the terms to research. Find out:
- what the hazard is;
- how it forms and works;
- how it affects living and non-living things;
- what steps citizens can take to prepare for such hazards;
- what people can do to protect themselves once the hazard starts;
- where people can get further information.

Here are some of the factors you could consider when assessing potential earthquake hazards for a particular area, or designing an investigation into earthquake hazards:
- closeness to active earthquake faults;
- seismic history of the region (how often earthquakes occur; time since last earthquake);
- building construction (type of building and foundation; architectural layout; materials used; quality of workmanship; extent to which earthquake resistance was considered by the designer);
- local conditions (type and condition of soil; slope of the land; fill material; geologic structure of the earth beneath; annual rainfall).

P
63

4. Digging Deeper
Scientists build on knowledge that others have discovered through investigation. In this section you can read about the insights scientists have about the question you are investigating. The questions in **As You Read** will help you focus on the information you are looking for.

5. Review and Reflect
After you have completed each investigation, you will be asked to reflect on what you have learned and how it relates to the "Big Picture" of the Earth system. You will also be asked to think about what scientific inquiry processes you used.

6. Investigation: Putting It All Together
In the last investigation of the module you will have a chance to "put it all together." You will be asked to apply all that you have learned in the previous investigations to solve a practical problem. This module is just the beginning! You continue to learn about the Earth system every time you ask questions and make observations about the world around you.

The Earth System

The Earth System is a set of systems that work together in making the world we know. Four of these important systems are:

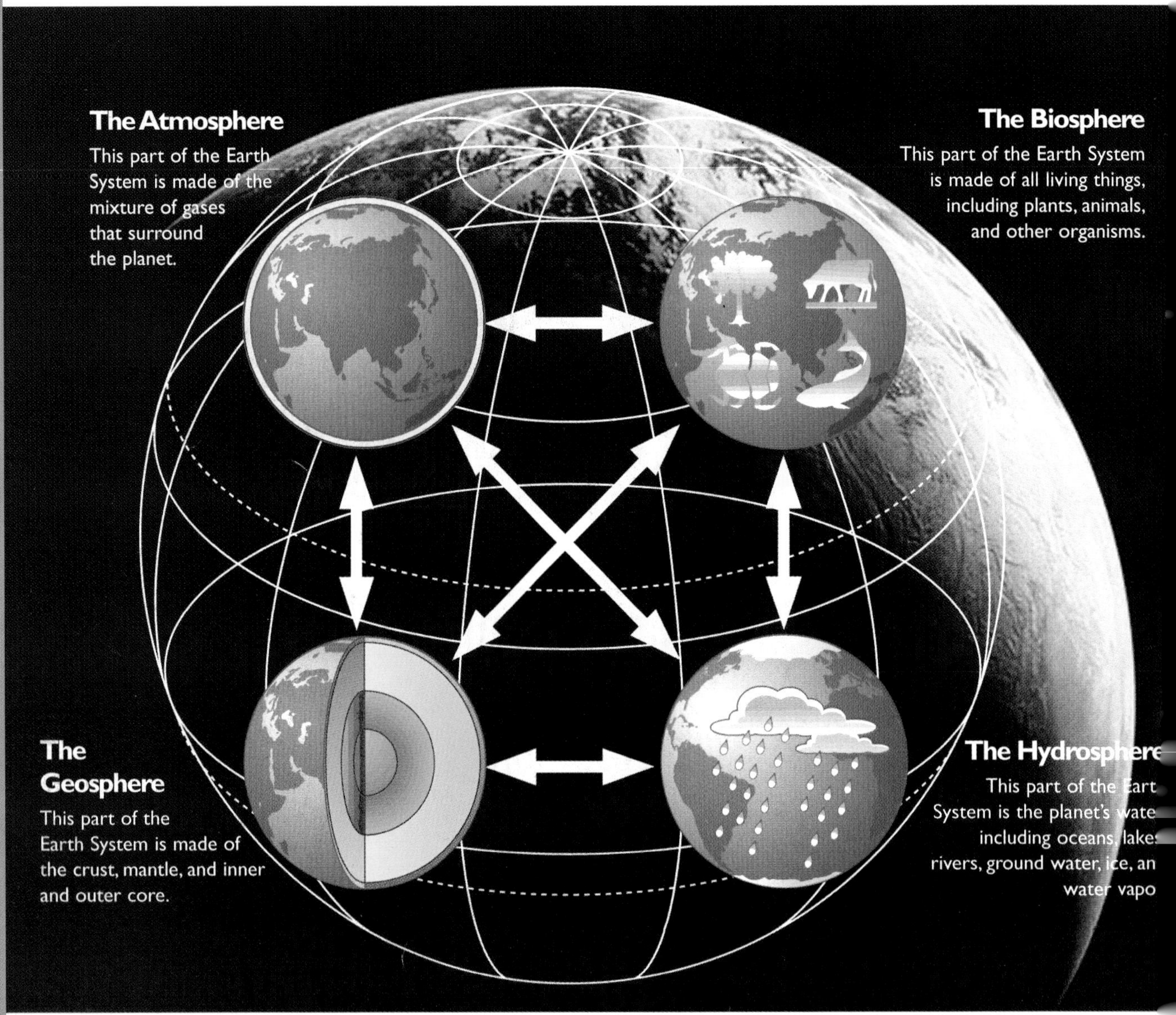

The Atmosphere

This part of the Earth System is made of the mixture of gases that surround the planet.

The Biosphere

This part of the Earth System is made of all living things, including plants, animals, and other organisms.

The Geosphere

This part of the Earth System is made of the crust, mantle, and inner and outer core.

The Hydrosphere

This part of the Eart System is the planet's wate including oceans, lake rivers, ground water, ice, an water vapo

These systems, and others, have been working together since the Earth's beginning more than 4.5 billion years ago. They are still working, because the Earth is always changing, even though we cannot always observe these changes. Energy from within and outside the Earth leads to changes in the Earth System. Changes in any one of these systems affects the others. This is why we think of the Earth as made of interrelated systems.

During your investigations, keep the Earth System in mind. At the end of each investigation you will be asked to think about how the things you have discovered fit with the Earth System.

To further understand the Earth System, take a look at THE BIG PICTURE shown on page 72.

Introducing Inquiry Processes

When geologists and other scientists investigate the world, they use a set of inquiry processes. Using these processes is very important. They ensure that the research is valid and reliable. In your investigations, you will use these same processes. In this way, you will become a scientist, doing what scientists do. Understanding inquiry processes will help you to investigate questions and solve problems in an orderly way. You will also use inquiry processes in high school, in college, and in your work.

During this module, you will learn when, and how, to use these inquiry processes. Use the chart below as a reference about the inquiry processes.

Inquiry Processes:	**How scientists use these processes**
Explore questions to answer by inquiry	Scientists usually form a question to investigate after first looking at what is known about a scientific idea. Sometimes they predict the most likely answer to a question. They base this prediction on what they already know to be true.
Design an investigation	To make sure that the way they test ideas is fair, scientists think very carefully about the design of their investigations. They do this to make sure that the results will be valid and reliable.
Conduct an investigation	After scientists have designed an investigation, they conduct their tests. They observe what happens and record the results. Often, they repeat a test several times to ensure reliable results.
Collect and review data using tools	Scientists collect information (data) from their tests. The data may be numerical (numbers), or verbal (words). To collect and manage data, scientists use tools such as computers, calculators, tables, charts, and graphs.
Use evidence to develop ideas	Evidence is very important for scientists. Just as in a court case, it is proven evidence that counts. Scientists look at the evidence other scientists have collected, as well as the evidence they have collected themselves.
Consider evidence for explanations	Finding strong evidence does not always provide the complete answer to a scientific question. Scientists look for likely explanations by studying patterns and relationships within the evidence.
Seek alternative explanations	Sometimes, the evidence available is not clear or can be interpreted in other ways. If this is so, scientists look for different ways of explaining the evidence. This may lead to a new idea or question to investigate.
Show evidence & reasons to others	Scientists communicate their findings to other scientists to see if they agree. Other scientists may then try to repeat the investigation to validate the results.
Use mathematics for science inquiry	Scientists use mathematics in their investigations. Accurate measurement, with suitable units is very important for both collecting and analyzing data. Data often consist of numbers and calculations.

Introducing Our Dynamic Planet

Have you ever seen a volcano erupting?

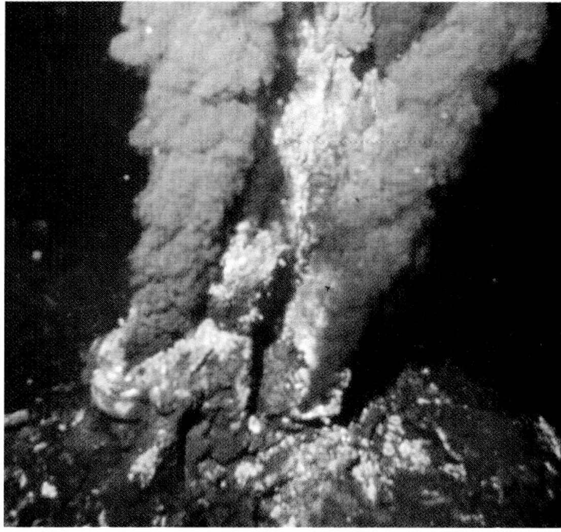

Have you ever heard about hydrothermal vents on the floor of the ocean?

Have you ever wondered how mountains form?

Have you ever seen the effect of an earthquake on a community?

Why Is Our Dynamic Planet Important?

Dynamic means powerful or active. Our dynamic planet is a powerful, active, ever-changing planet. Powerful events like earthquakes and volcanic eruptions have been happening since the Earth formed, over 4.5 billion years ago. Every feature of our planet changes, on time scales that range from minutes to millions of years. The deepest oceans, the highest mountain peaks—all represent but a page in the volume of Earth's history. Mountains have been destroyed, recycled, and reborn. Oceans have risen and fallen.

These processes are still at work today. Knowledge about present-day volcanic eruptions and earthquakes give clues about the past. Rocks, landforms, and fossils also provide evidence of a long and varied history of the Earth. Knowing about our dynamic planet will help you to understand the past and prepare for the future.

What Will You Investigate?

You will look for evidence and help solve some of the puzzles surrounding Earth processes. Here are some of the things that you will investigate:

- how scientists make and use models;
- what the inside of the Earth is like;
- how the Earth's surface moves;
- how mountains form;
- what causes earthquakes.

You will need to practice your problem-solving skills. You will also need to be good observers and recorders, as you work together with other members of your class.

In the last investigation you will have a chance to apply all that you have learned about our dynamic planet. You will investigate a natural hazard in depth. Then you will design a brochure to provide information to residents of a community on how to prepare for, and protect against, natural disasters.

Investigation 1:

Gathering Evidence and Modeling

Key Question

Before you begin, first think about this key question.

How do you make a model of something that you cannot see?

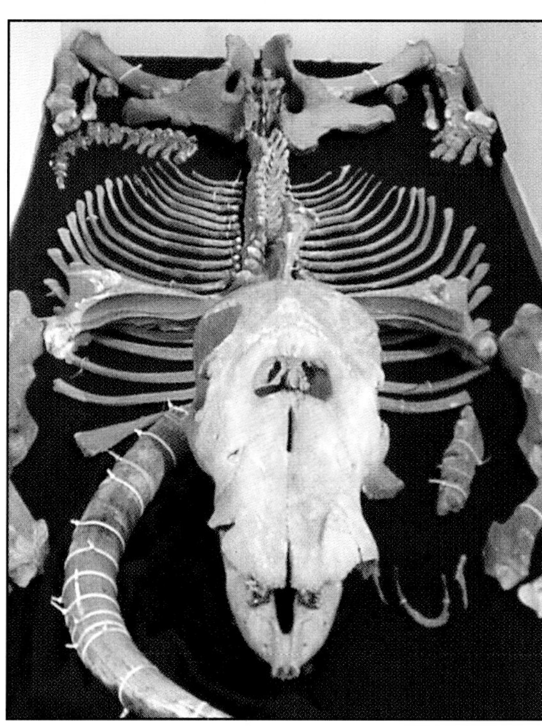

Think about what you know about models. What are some models of things or processes that cannot be seen with the naked eye? How do you think these models were constructed?

Discuss the key question with your group and your class. Record your thoughts in your journal. Be prepared to share your thinking with the rest of the class.

Materials Needed

For this investigation your group will need:

- double-bagged, brown paper bag with "mystery objects" sealed inside
- colored pencils

Investigate

1. Several kinds of objects have been placed into a brown paper "mystery bag," and it has been sealed shut. You will use three senses (smell, hearing, and touch) to gather data about the bag's contents. Then you will design new tests to get more information.

In your journal, write your research question: "What are the contents of the Mystery Bag?" Underneath your research question, write your prediction.

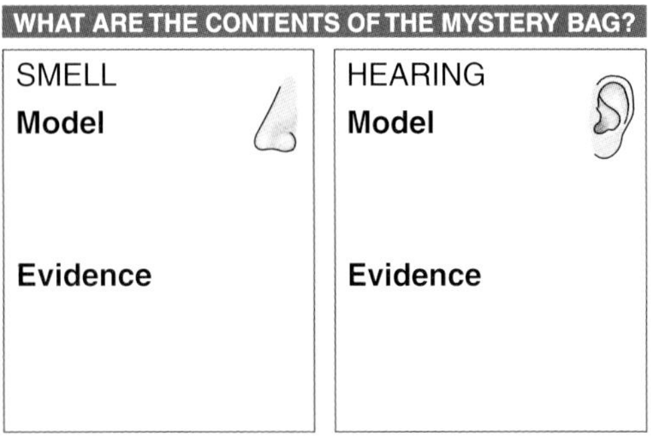
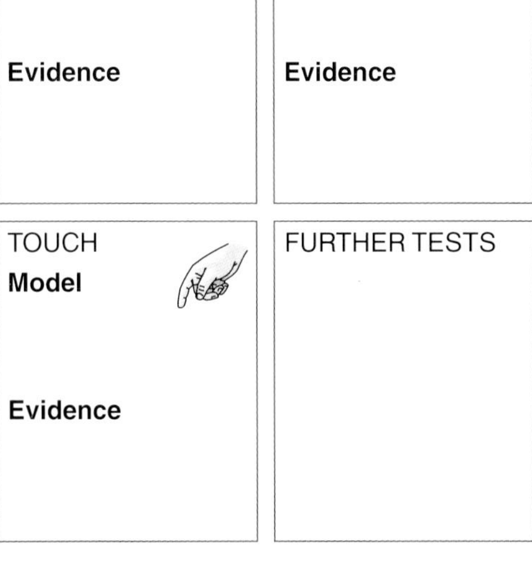

2. Divide a sheet of paper into four equal sections. Label the four sections as follows:
    - Smell
    - Hearing
    - Touch
    - Further Tests

    Divide the sections for smell, hearing, and touch, into two sections: model and evidence. In the evidence section you will write observations that support your ideas about what you think is in the bag. In the model section you will draw a model of what you think is in the bag.

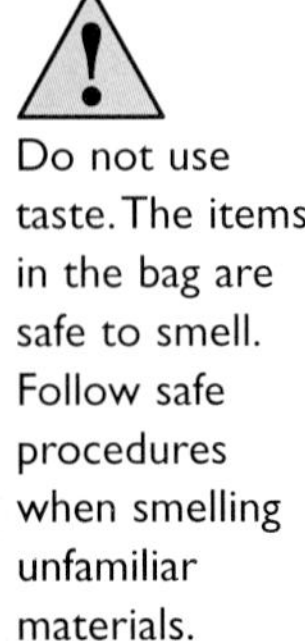

Do not use taste. The items in the bag are safe to smell. Follow safe procedures when smelling unfamiliar materials.

3. The first sense you will use is smell. Your teacher will place the bag on the center of your table. Smell the bag without touching it.
   a) Record your ideas about what is in the bag in the "model" section of the square, using pictures.
   b) In the other section of the box, record your evidence. This is like a justification, or explanation, of why you drew the picture the way you did.
4. Next, you will use your sense of hearing. One member of your group should pick up the bag and shake it, while walking around to each group member.
   a) Record your model(s) in the correct square, using pictures.
   b) Record your evidence.
5. Next, you will use your sense of touch, using care not to open or damage the bag, or the bag's contents. Allow each group member to touch the bag.
   a) Record your model(s) in the correct square, using pictures.
   b) Record your evidence.
6. Discuss your models and evidence in your group.

   When you have come to an agreement, select a group member to share one of your group's models and evidence with the rest of the class.
7. After discussing your class's findings, compose a list of further tests you could perform to gather more evidence. These do not have to be tests that you will actually try in the classroom, although they could be. The only rule is that you may not look inside the bag.
   a) Write your group's ideas under "Further Tests" in your journal.
   b) Share your ideas in a group discussion.

Inquiry

Using Evidence

Evidence is very important for scientists. They can use evidence to develop conceptual models (what they think something they cannot see might look like). Evidence comes from observation and data. In this investigation you can use the data you collect from your observations as evidence to develop a conceptual model of what is in the brown paper bag.

Have your teacher check your tests for safety if you plan on trying any of them. Wash your hands after the activity.

Digging  Deeper

MODELS

As You Read...
Think about:

1. *What is the difference between a physical model and a conceptual model?*
2. *What is the difference between a hypothesis and a model?*
3. *How does mathematics help in developing models?*
4. *How do computers help in developing models?*

In science there are many kinds of models. Scientists use the words "model" and "modeling" in many different ways.

Physical Models

Physical models are structures that scientists build to represent something else. This kind of model is probably what would pop into your mind first if somebody asked you what a model is. The simplest kind of physical model is just a small-scale structure of what a much larger item looks like, or once looked like but no longer exists. The dinosaurs you might see in a museum are models built by paleontologists (scientists who study fossils and ancient life). They collect the fossilized bones and then make plaster casts of them. They try to fit the bones together in the most realistic way. Then they try to imagine what the flesh and skin might have looked like.

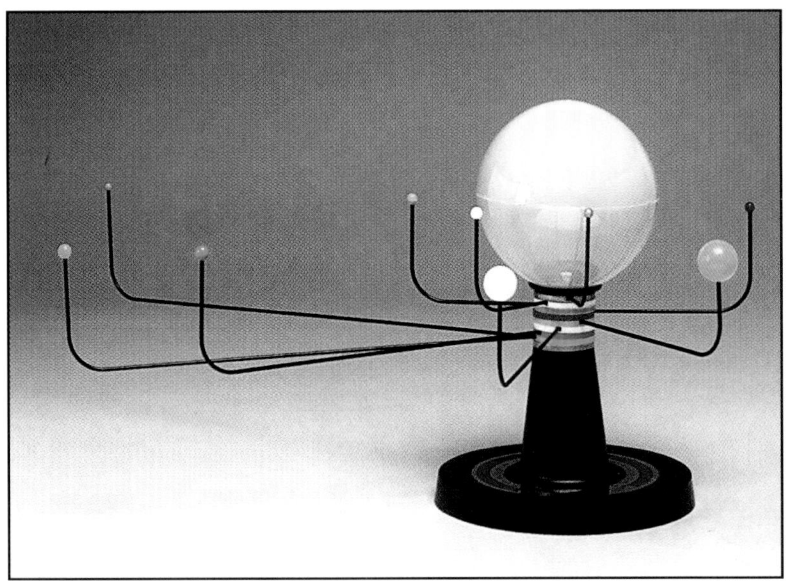

Other physical models simulate some event or process in nature. Very large-scale natural processes like river-flow or ocean waves are difficult to study in the outdoors. Scientists build tanks, channels, or basins to reproduce the processes in a laboratory. Sometimes they are able to adjust the conditions (things like speed of water-flow, or the behavior of water waves). Then what they observe in the model represents what happens in the outdoors. Even if they are not able to do that, then at least they are able to get some valuable qualitative data just by watching what happens in the model.

Conceptual Models

Conceptual models are models that scientists develop in their minds. Scientists often try to develop a concept about how some process works in nature. The basis for the concept is what has already been observed about the process, together with what the scientist knows about basic physical or chemical laws. A conceptual model is a bit like a hypothesis. It is usually broader than a hypothesis, however, because it deals with many things about a complicated natural system. A good example of a conceptual model is the picture scientists have about the nature of atoms. You probably know that atoms consist of a nucleus, and electrons that orbit around the nucleus. The nucleus consists of protons and neutrons. That's the simplest conceptual model of an atom. With the discovery of even more elementary particles, that original conceptual model of an atom has been enlarged and extended.

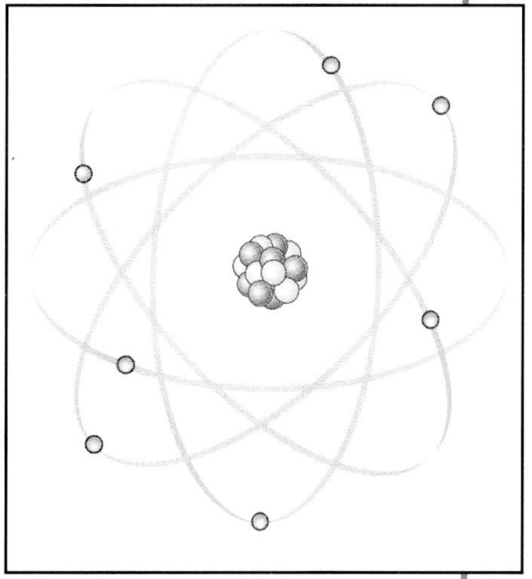

Inquiry

Hypotheses

A hypothesis is a testable statement or idea about how something works. It is based on what you think that you know or understand already. A hypothesis is never a guess. You test a hypothesis by comparing it to observations or data that already exist or that can be gathered in the future. A hypothesis forms the basis for making a prediction, and is used to design an experiment or observation to find out more about a scientific idea or question. Guesses can be useful in science, but they are not hypotheses.

Mathematical Models

Sometimes, scientists are able to write mathematical equations that describe how some process works. The equations express basic physical and chemical laws. Then they solve the equations, in the same way that students in a math class solve equations. The solutions to the equations tell how the process will work, under a variety of conditions. This allows scientists to predict what will happen—which is one of the important things scientists try to do.

Numerical Models

Sometimes, scientists are able to develop a mathematical model, but the model would take too long to fully test by hand. That's where high-speed computers come in. The equations are programmed into the computer. The computer can then compute the model thousands of times. In this way it can quickly simulate what happens either over time, or with changing conditions. As computing power has grown in recent years, the ability of computers to handle numerical models has gotten much greater. Several groups of climatologists (scientists who study global climate) have developed numerical models to study how the Earth's climate might change in the coming decades. As more and more is known about processes of climate, the models are continually being refined.

Review and Reflect

Review

1. Look again at the **Key Question** for this investigation. In your journal, write down what you have learned from your investigation that provides answers.
2. Describe how and why your third model (using touch) is a better model than your first model (using smell).
3. Of the four kinds of models described in the **Digging Deeper** reading section, how would you classify your model of the mystery bag? Explain your answer.

Reflect

4. Explain how time and cost considerations might affect the process of making a model.
5. How does technology affect the ability of scientists to develop models?
6. Describe a situation in which a model is made of something that cannot be observed directly. Use an example that has not been given in this investigation.

Thinking about the Earth System

7. The modeling that you did with the mystery bag can be connected to the Earth's major systems. Provide a connection to each of the Earth systems in this investigation. Remember to write connections, as you find them, on the *Earth System Connection* sheet.

Thinking about Scientific Inquiry

8. What role did evidence play in your group's models?
9. How was communicating findings to others an important scientific process in this activity?
10. In what ways would the process of making a model of the Earth's interior be like the mystery bag activity?

Investigation 2:

The Interior of the Earth

Key Question

Before you begin, first think about this key question.

What is the interior of the Earth like?

Materials Needed

For this part of the investigation your group will need:

- large, flat-bottomed container
- black permanent marker
- plastic metric ruler – 30 cm
- pebble about one centimeter in diameter
- flashlight
- stopwatch

You now understand how sensory observations and experiments provide the basis for models. Make a drawing of what you think the interior of the Earth is like. What measurements, observations, or instruments would give scientists evidence about the Earth's interior?

Discuss your drawing and your thinking with your group and your class.

Investigate

Part A: Observing Waves and Measuring Wave Speed

1. With the permanent black marker, make a clearly visible dot near one end of the bottom of a container. Make another clearly visible dot near the other end of the container. Measure the distance between the dots, in centimeters.

   a) Record the distance in your journal.

2. Pour water into the container to a depth of 2 to 3 cm. Let the water come to rest, until the water surface is mirror smooth.
3. Have one student hold a pebble 5 cm over one of the marks on the bottom of the container.
4. Have a second student shine a flashlight beam straight down on the other mark. This student should lean directly over the flashlight to see the reflection of the beam from the water surface. This student should also hold a stopwatch and be familiar with how it works.
5. While the second student stares carefully at the reflection of the flashlight beam, the first student drops the pebble into the water. The second student starts the stopwatch when he or she hears the pebble enter the water. The second student stops the watch when he or she first detects motion of the water in the flashlight beam. This motion signals the arrival of the wave.

a) Record the time on the stopwatch as the travel time of the wave.

Inquiry

Conducting an Investigation

After scientists have designed an investigation, they conduct their test. The test must be free from uncontrolled variables. In this case you must be sure that the pebble is dropped from the same height each time, and the stopwatch is started and stopped at the correct time. Tests are often repeated several times to ensure reliable and valid results.

Wear goggles when dropping the pebble. Wash your hands after the activity.

6. Repeat the measurements until your group has at least 10 measurements. If one or two of the measurements are very different from all of the others, they are probably what a scientist would call a "gross error." You can ignore a few bad measurements like that, but be sure you have a large number of "good" measurements.

7. Calculate the average travel time. Add up all the measured travel times and then divide the sum by the number of measurements. Be sure to not include the bad measurements.

   a) In your journal, record the average travel time.

8. Calculate the wave speed in centimeters per second. Use the following equation:

$$\textbf{average wave speed (cm/s)} = \frac{\textbf{distance between dots (cm)}}{\textbf{average travel time (s)}}$$

   a) Record your calculations and your result in your journal.

Inquiry

Using Mathematics

Scientists use mathematics in their investigations. Accurate measurement, with suitable units, is very important when collecting data. In this investigation you made measurements. You then used the measurements to make calculations to interpret the data you collected.

9. Suppose you had a long pan of water. How long would it take the waves to travel:

   a) 50 cm?

   b) 100 cm?

   c) 200 cm?

10. Suppose you dropped stones into a material through which waves move twice as fast as they do through water.

    a) How would this change the average travel time of the waves?

11. Scientists cannot observe earthquake waves moving through the Earth in the same way you can observe waves moving through water. They can, however, record and study the energy from earthquake waves as the waves arrive at a recording station (seismograph station). They can use information they record about the waves to make models of the interior of the Earth.

    Think about how what you studied relates to how scientists make models of the inside of the Earth. What part of your experiment represented:

    a) An earthquake, which releases energy in the Earth?

    b) The movement of energy waves from the earthquakes (seismic waves) in the Earth?

c) The material in the Earth through which seismic waves travel?

d) The arrival of a seismic wave at a seismograph station where earthquakes are detected?

12. Compare your average travel time with those of other groups. Discuss the following questions and record the results of your discussions:

a) What might cause differences in travel times from measurement to measurement within your group?

b) What might cause differences in average travel times among the different groups?

c) What improvements to your measurement technique might decrease the difference in values you obtained?

Part B: Kinds of Seismic Waves

1. With a partner, stretch out a Slinky® on the floor about as far as it can go without making a permanent bend in the metal.

2. Have one partner make waves by holding the end of the Slinky with a fist, and striking the fist with the other hand, directly toward the end of the Slinky.

Observe the direction of wave movement, relative to the Slinky.

a) Does it move in the same direction (parallel to the Slinky) or in the opposite direction (perpendicular to the Slinky)? Record your observation in your journal.

b) This kind of wave is called a compressional wave. (To compress means to squeeze together.) From your observations, explain why this is an appropriate name for this wave. You may wish to use diagrams to illustrate your answer.

Materials Needed

For this part of the investigation your group will need:

• two Slinkys®

Wear safety goggles throughout. Be sure that neither partner holding the Slinky lets go while it is stretched out. Wash your hands after the activity.

3. Stretch out the Slinky again. This time, have one partner make waves by moving the Slinky from side to side (left to right or right to left).

   Again, observe the direction of wave movement, relative to the Slinky.

   a) Does the wave move in the same direction (parallel to the Slinky) or in the opposite direction (perpendicular to the Slinky)? Record your observation in your journal.

   b) This kind of wave is called a shear wave. (To shear means to slide one thing sideways past another thing.) From your observations, explain why this is an appropriate name for this wave. You may wish to use diagrams to illustrate your answer.

A stretched Slinky can move unpredictably when released. Spread out so that you can work without hitting anyone. Do not release the Slinky while it is stretched. Walk together until the Slinky is not stretched and then have one person take both ends to put it away.

4. To compare the two types of wave motions, stretch out two Slinkys along the floor, about 5 m.

   Starting at the same end at the same time, have one student holding the end of the Slinky strike their fist. Have another student jerk the other Slinky back and forth. Observe what happens.

   Try the movements several times until you are confident in your observations.

   a) Which of the two wave types arrives at the other end first (which one is faster)? Explain why you think this happens.

Part C: Refraction of Waves

In **Part A**, you investigated the speed of waves as they pass through one kind of material (water). In **Part B**, you saw that different kinds of waves have different speeds. Next, you will simulate what happens when a seismic wave crosses a boundary between two kinds of materials. It will help if you read all the steps below before you do the activity.

Materials Needed

For this part of the investigation your group will need:

- large open floor area (paved parking lot or playground)
- piece of white chalk (or masking tape)
- piece of red chalk
- clear container
- long pencil

1. One person will be the "marker." That person holds the pieces of chalk. The marker should draw two lines:
   - A long, straight line in white chalk across the middle of the area. The white line represents a boundary between two layers in the Earth.
   - A long straight line in red chalk at a 20° angle to the white chalk line. The red line represents the front of a seismic wave that is moving through the Earth.

The marker should also draw an arrow about one meter long and perpendicular to the red chalk line. The result should look like the diagram shown.

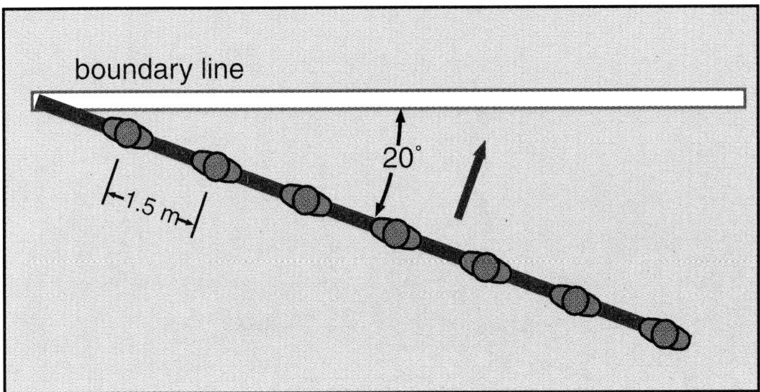

2. Form a line of students along the red line. Stand about 1.5 m apart from one another (arm's length apart).
3. When the marker gives the signal to start, everybody in the line moves forward, taking steps 30 cm long every second. Walk straight ahead as shown by the arrow in the diagram.
4. The instant you cross the white line, keep walking straight ahead, but start to take steps one meter long instead of small steps.
5. After the last person has reached the white chalk line, the marker will tell everybody to stop walking.
6. With the red chalk, the marker will make a long, straight chalk line just in front of everyone's toes. The new red line should connect to the white chalk line. The marker should also draw an arrow about three feet long and perpendicular to the new red line.
7. Stand back and look at the two red chalk lines. Compare the angle of the new red chalk line with that of the old red chalk line.
8. Obtain a copy of the diagram shown above.
   a) Label the region above the boundary "wave speed = 1 m/s" and the layer below the boundary "wave speed = 30 cm/s."
   b) The diagram already shows the old red chalk line. Add the new red line from your results to the diagram. Try to draw the angle accurately, but do not worry if it is not exact.

c) Does the second red chalk line form a different angle with the white chalk line, or the same angle?

d) What is the basic reason for the difference in the angles of the red chalk lines?

e) If the speed of a seismic wave increased after it crossed a boundary in the Earth, what do you think would happen to the wave?

9. With your group, devise a plan to investigate a different kind of change in wave speed. For example, in the original activity, the waves moved (roughly) 30 cm/s and then moved 1 m/s after they crossed the boundary. What would happen if the waves slowed down after crossing the boundary? What would happen if the waves moved four times as fast after crossing the boundary? How would this affect the path of the wave?

a) In your journal, record what you plan to investigate.

b) Predict how you think this would this change the angle of the second red line. Include the reason for your prediction.

Have your plan checked by your teacher before you begin.

c) Record your prediction on a second copy of the diagram. Label the diagram to indicate the relative speeds of waves before and after the boundary.

10. Repeat the activity.

a) Record your observations in your journal by drawing the angle of the new red line.

b) How does the angle of the new red line compare with your prediction?

Clean up spills immediately.

11. Fill a clear container almost full of water. Put the pencil halfway into the water, at an angle. Look at the pencil from above, but slightly to the side.

a) Draw a picture of what you observe.

b) Do you think that light waves travel at the same speed through water as they do through air, or at different speeds? Explain your answer. Relate this to what you discovered about the bending of waves in **Part C.**

12. Imagine a liquid in which light waves travel twice as fast as they do through water.

a) Draw a picture of what the pencil would look like if it were put into this liquid. Explain your drawing.

Part D: Refraction of Earthquake Waves in the Earth

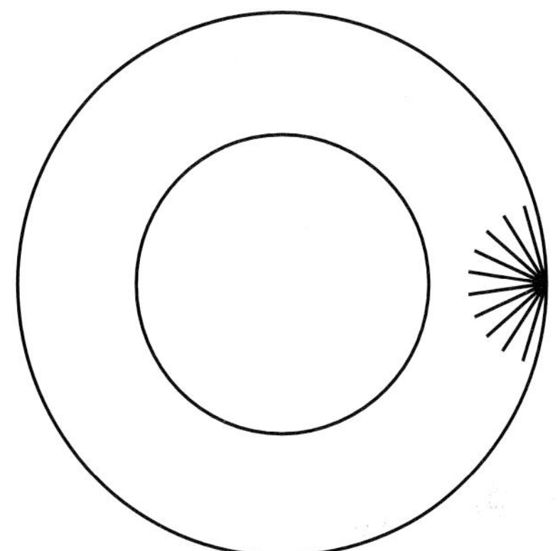

1. Obtain a copy of a diagram similar to the one shown.

   The large circle represents the Earth. The small circle represents the edge of an inner part of the Earth where earthquake waves move faster than in the outer part. The black dot near the right-hand edge of the large circle represents a place in the Earth where an earthquake happens.

2. The earthquake sends seismic waves in all directions through the Earth. Notice the short lines coming from the dot. These lines show the start of some of the directions in which the waves start to travel (like the arrow that you drew in **Part C**). Your challenge is to show how these directions change when the wave goes through different layers of the Earth.

3. Use your straightedge and pencil to extend the lines through the Earth to the other side. Think about the following before you begin:

   - Some of the lines will go through the Earth without hitting the inner circle.
   - Some of the lines, however, will hit the inner circle. This is a boundary between zones with different wave speeds. From **Part C** of the investigation, when you pretended you were part of a wave, you then learned what happens.
   - The lines that go into the inner circle also come out of the inner circle. When that happens, the waves will be crossing a boundary again. Think about what will happen to their direction of travel.

4. When you have completed all of the lines, look at where they are when they reach the other side of the Earth.

   a) Describe the pattern shown by the waves when they reach the other side of the Earth.

Materials Needed

For this part of the investigation your group will need:

- pencil with a good eraser
- transparent straightedge or ruler

b) How does the pattern help you to understand how scientists in another part of the Earth can detect an earthquake?

c) How does this help you to understand why scientists in some places would not be able to detect some of the earthquake waves?

d) Scientists used this pattern to argue that the Earth has a core. They claimed that it showed that seismic waves pass through a zone with different wave speeds. Does this conclusion make sense? Explain why or why not.

Digging  Deeper

As You Read...
Think about:

1. ***What is the difference between compressional (P) waves and shear (S) waves?***
2. ***How do earthquakes produce seismic waves?***
3. ***How would you describe wave refraction?***
4. ***What is the focus of an earthquake?***
5. ***How are earthquake waves detected on the surface of the Earth?***
6. ***How do scientists know that the Earth's mantle is made of solid rock?***
7. ***How do scientists know that the Earth has a core?***

WHAT EARTHQUAKE WAVES REVEAL ABOUT THE INTERIOR OF THE EARTH

Waves

Shaking a material produces vibrations. Those vibrations move away in all directions in the form of a wave. You saw that clearly with the Slinky®. Speech is another good example. When you speak, you are making your vocal cords vibrate. That makes the air around them vibrate. The vibrations travel out from your mouth and through the air as sound waves. As the waves travel, they carry energy with them. The water waves you made in the pan were given their energy by the falling stone. The waves then delivered their energy to the sides of the pan.

The first kind of wave you made with the Slinky is called a compressional wave. When you compressed (squeezed together) the end of the Slinky by hitting it with your fist, it tried to expand again, and when it did, it compressed the material next to it. That part of the coil then expanded again, and so on. The wave of compression and expansion traveled along the coil as a wave.

The second kind of wave you made with the Slinky is called a shear wave. When you moved the Slinky sideways, it pulled the material next to it sideways as well. In turn, that material pulled the next part of the Slinky sideways, and so on down the length of the Slinky.

Earthquakes and Seismic Waves

During an earthquake, large masses of rock slide past each other, making powerful vibrations. That also happens in human-made explosions. The vibrations move away in all directions through the Earth in the form of waves, called seismic waves. The seismic waves travel all the way through the Earth. When they reach the Earth's surface again, they can be detected with special instruments called seismographs. There are hundreds of seismograph stations all around the Earth.

The Richter Scale is a way of measuring the magnitude of an earthquake using seismograph records. Each whole number increase on the Richter Scale is an increase of 10 times in the size of the vibrations recorded and an increase of 31 times the amount of energy released! To give you some idea of the different magnitudes, anything less than a magnitude 2.5 is too small to be felt by humans. A magnitude 4.5 or over is capable of causing damage near the earthquake, and anything over a magnitude 7 is considered a major earthquake that is potentially very destructive.

Seismic waves weaken as they move through the Earth. That is why the distance from the earthquake must also be considered when calculating the Richter magnitude. There are two reasons that the seismic waves weaken. They spread their energy over a larger and larger area, just like the ripples in the pan of water. Also, they lose energy because they create some friction as they move through the Earth.

Wave Refraction

You saw in **Part C** of the investigation how a wave (the line of students) changes its direction when it suddenly passes from a material with low wave speed ("short steps") to a material with high wave speed ("long steps"). The change in direction is called refraction. Refraction also happens where the wave speed changes gradually rather than suddenly. Suppose you were in a marching band, and the leader yells, "Members on the right take giant steps, members on the left take small steps." You can imagine what would happen. The whole line would gradually curve more and more to the left. The same kind of thing happens with seismic waves in the Earth. The speed of seismic waves generally increases downward in the mantle, so the path of a wave curves upward as the wave passes through the mantle (see the diagram).

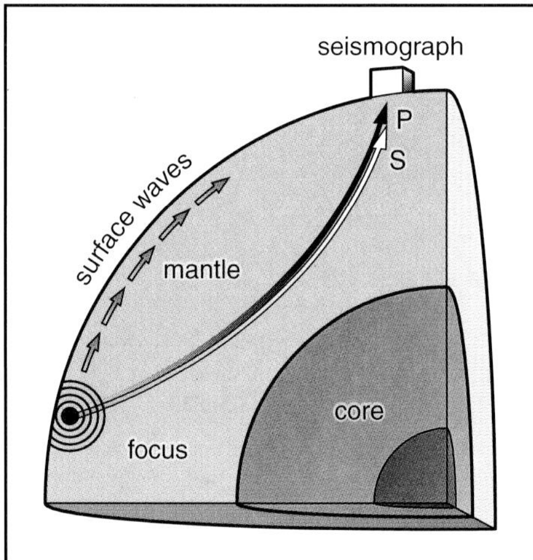

The reason why the speed of seismic waves increases downward in the mantle is complicated, but scientists are able to measure the seismic-wave speed of rocks in the laboratory using special equipment. Using this equipment they can determine how differences in temperature, pressure, and the type of rock affect the speed of seismic waves.

The Interior of the Earth

The main way that scientists know about the interior of the Earth is by studying how seismic waves pass through it. In **Part D** of the investigation, you showed something important about the interior of the Earth. Long ago, scientists noticed that there is a zone where seismic waves from a faraway earthquake do not appear again at the surface. This zone is in the form of a large ring on the Earth's surface, as shown in the diagram. This ring is called

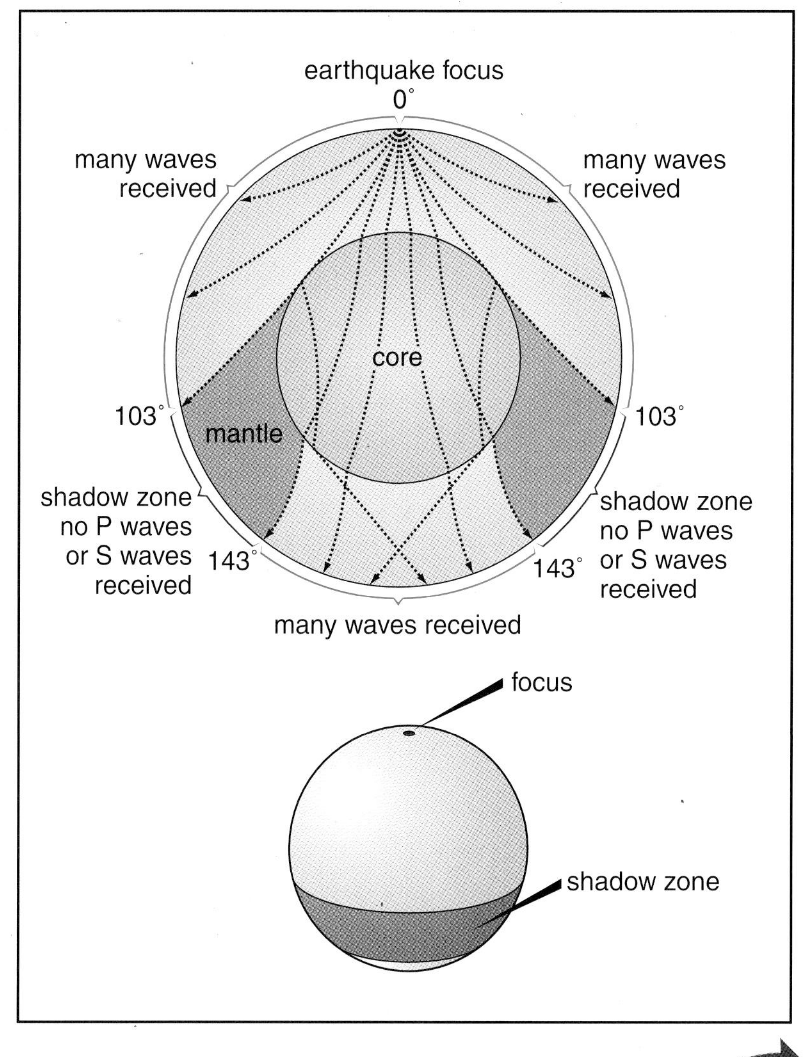

the "shadow zone." This shows that there is a place deep inside of the Earth where there is an abrupt slowing of seismic-wave speeds. How can this be if the seismic-wave speed of the mantle increases with depth? The answer is that there must be an inner shell of the Earth (called the core) that is made of a material that is very different from the mantle.

The core almost certainly consists mostly of iron. You probably know, from using a compass, that the Earth has a strong magnetic field. The only way the Earth can have a magnetic field is for the core to be made of iron. The outer part of the Earth, above the core, is called the mantle. It consists of mostly solid rock. Remember from **Part B** of the investigation that two kinds of seismic waves can go through the Earth: compressional (P) waves, and shear (S) waves. It's known that P waves can pass through solids, liquids, and gases, but S waves can go only through solids. Both P waves and S waves go through the mantle, so it must be solid. On the other hand, only P waves go through the core, so its iron must be melted rather than solid. There is even an inner core within the outer core. The inner core seems to be solid rather than liquid. Scientists discovered the inner core by some very careful detective work, long after the core itself had been discovered. The outermost layer of the Earth, above the mantle, is called the crust. The crust is very thin, not more than about 50 km thick. You will learn more about the Earth's crust in a later activity. The diagram shows the Earth's core, mantle, and crust.

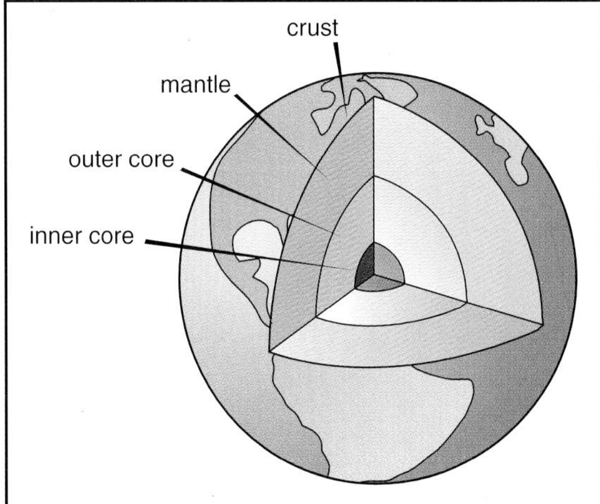

Review and Reflect

Review

1. The direction of wave motion and the direction that a wave travels or propagates are not necessarily the same thing. How were the two types of waves you made in **Part B** of the investigation different from one another?
2. Why do seismic waves follow a curved path through the Earth?
3. How do scientists know that the Earth's core is made of a different material than that of the mantle?

Reflect

4. Think about the **Key Question:** "What is the interior of the Earth like?" Has your answer to this question changed from the beginning of the investigation? Explain.
5. Give an example of how you used a model in this investigation.
6. What have you learned about how scientists investigate the Earth?

Thinking about the Earth System

7. On your *Earth System Connection* sheet, summarize what you have learned about the geosphere.
8. Suppose an earthquake occurred below the ocean floor. How might earthquakes affect the hydrosphere?

Thinking about Scientific Inquiry

9. How did you revise your ideas on the basis of evidence?
10. Why did you repeat the experiment (conduct multiple trials) in **Part A** of the investigation?

Investigation 3:

Forces that Cause Earth Movements

Key Question

Before you begin, first think about this key question.

Does the rock of the Earth's mantle move?

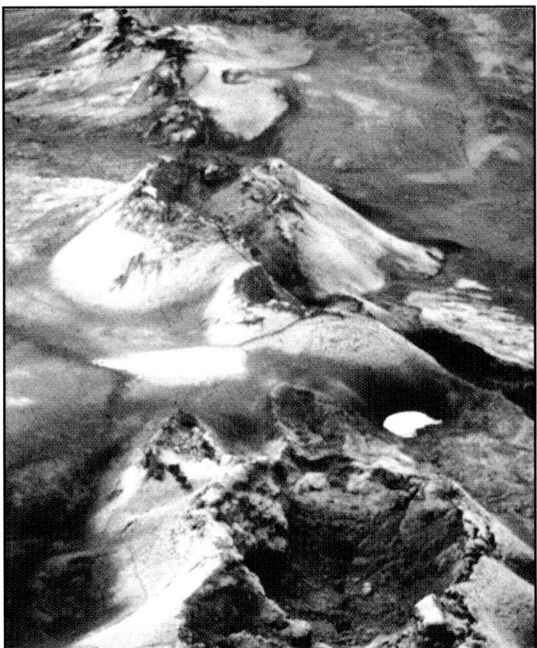

In the previous investigation you learned that the outer part of the Earth, above the core, is called the mantle. It consists mostly of solid rock. Is it possible that this rock moves?

Share your thinking with others in your class. Keep a record of the discussion in your journal.

Materials Needed

For this investigation, each group will need:

- candle
- small heat-resistant container
- corn syrup
- two pieces of thin cardboard, 1 cm square
- two small bricks
- lighter or matches

Investigate

1. Set up the experiment as shown on the opposite page. Place a small heat-resistant container where it can receive heat from a candle.

   Pour one centimeter of cold corn syrup into the container.

Place two pieces of cardboard so they touch, side by side, on top of the syrup in the center of the container.

2. Before you light the candle, predict what you think will happen to the cardboard as the corn syrup heats up.
   a) Record your prediction, and also the reason(s) for your prediction.
3. When you have had your equipment CHECKED FOR SAFETY, light the candle and slide it under the center of the container.
   a) While waiting for the corn syrup to heat, draw a side view of the container alongside your prediction and reason(s).
4. Watch carefully as the corn syrup heats up.
   a) Record your observations and interpretations in your journal.
   b) On your "side-view" drawing of the experimental setup, show any movement of the cardboard with solid arrows.
   c) Show the movement of the corn syrup with dashed arrows.
5. Next you will watch a demonstration.

   A clear, heat-proof beaker, two-thirds full with water is placed on a hot plate.

   When the water is simmering (not boiling), one cup of oatmeal will be poured into the beaker. One drop of food coloring will be added. Finally, some sawdust will be added.

Inquiry

Making Diagrams

Sometimes the best way to show the results of a scientific investigation is by drawing a diagram. Complicated concepts can often be illustrated more easily than they can be explained in words. The diagram should be labeled and described in a sentence or two.

Be careful with open flames. Tie back hair and push back or roll up loose clothing. Remove loose jewelry from near your hands. Wear goggles. Allow the syrup to cool completely before touching the heat-resistant container. Clean up spills immediately.

This is a demonstration only. Once the oatmeal is taken into the lab, it must be considered contaminated because it is used in a science activity. Do not consume the oatmeal.

a) Write a prediction about what you think will happen to oatmeal, food coloring and sawdust when they are added to the water. Give a reason for your prediction.

When the hot plate is turned on and the water begins to warm, carefully observe what happens when oatmeal, food coloring, and sawdust are added.

b) Describe what you observe. Draw a series of diagrams to record your observations.

6. Below is a simple cross-section diagram of a mid-ocean ridge, showing both what is above and below the Earth's surface.

Think about how the corn syrup model and the oatmeal model behaved, especially the cardboard and sawdust, as the liquid heats up. Compare this to the diagram.

a) What evidence can you find from your models that might be similar to what you see in the diagram?

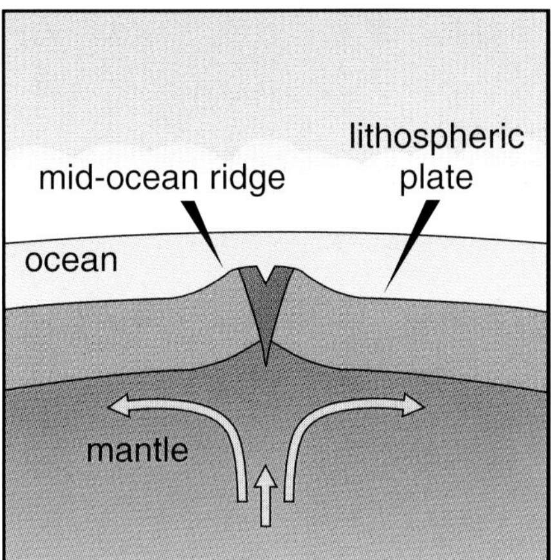

7. What parts or processes within the Earth do you think each of the following parts of your model represent?

a) the heat source;

b) the upward movement of water/syrup;

c) the horizontal movement of water/syrup;

d) the separation of the cardboard by syrup;

e) the horizontal movement of the cardboard/sawdust.

8. Hold a whole-class session where each group in turn posts and explains its diagrams to others. Look for similarities and differences and try to reach some overall agreements about the Atlantic's mid-ocean ridge.

Digging  Deeper

FORCES THAT DRIVE OUR DYNAMIC PLANET

Convection Cells

Convection is a motion in a fluid that is caused by heating from below and cooling from above. The corn syrup and oatmeal in your investigation were convecting. When a liquid is heated, it expands slightly. That makes its density slightly less. The fluid with lower density then rises up, in the same way that a party balloon filled with helium rises up. With the balloon, you can even feel the upward tug on the string! When the heated liquid reaches cool surroundings, it shrinks again, making its density greater. It then sinks down toward where it was first heated. This circulation, which you observed in the corn syrup, and in the water/oatmeal mixture, is called a convection cell.

As You Read...
Think about:
1. ***What are the conditions that cause convection cells in a fluid?***
2. ***How can the mantle convect if it is a solid?***
3. ***What is the typical speed of mantle convection?***
4. ***What is the reason for volcanic activity along mid-ocean ridges?***
5. ***What kinds of forces drive sea-floor spreading?***

Convection in the Earth's Mantle

In **Investigation 2** you learned that the Earth's mantle extends down to the hot iron core. It is known that P waves can pass through solids, liquids, and gases, but S waves can go only through solids. Both P waves and S waves go through the mantle, so it must be solid. On the other hand, only P waves go through the core, so its iron must be melted rather than solid. Scientists are now sure that the mantle convects, in the form of gigantic convection cells. How can that be, if the mantle is solid rock?

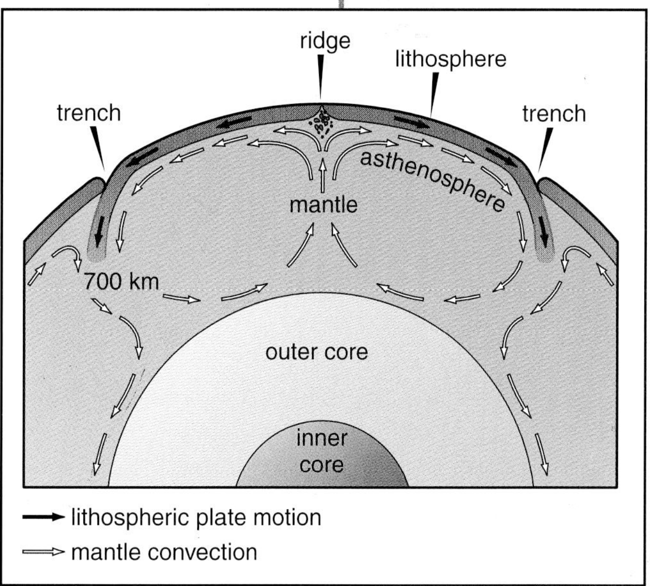

Many materials act like solids on short time scales but like liquids on much longer time scales. If you've ever played with Silly Putty®, you know all about that. Ordinary glass is also a good example. You know that it breaks easily. But if you were to take a long glass rod and hang it horizontally between two supports, it would gradually sag down in the middle. It would have flowed, to take on a new shape, even though it seems like a solid. The Earth's mantle behaves in just the same way. The speeds of flow in the mantle are only a few centimeters per year, but over millions of years of geologic time, that adds up to a lot of movement. Here's a comparison that will give you a good idea of how fast the convection cells in the mantle move: about as fast as your fingernails grow!

The Lithosphere and the Asthenosphere

The outermost part of the Earth, down to a depth of 100 to 200 km in most places, is cooler than the deeper part of the Earth. Because this outermost part of the Earth is relatively cool, it stays rigid, and it does not take part in the convection of the mantle. It is called the lithosphere ("rock sphere"). The lithosphere is made up of the crust and the uppermost part of the mantle. Below the lithosphere is a zone where the mantle rocks are just hot enough and under enough pressure that they will deform and change shape. This zone is right below the lithosphere and is called the asthenosphere. You can think of the lithosphere as a rigid slab that rides on top of the convecting asthenosphere. That is much like the cardboard that rode on top of the syrup in your model. The lithosphere consists of several pieces, each in a different part of the world. These pieces are called lithospheric plates.

Mid-Ocean Ridges

All the Earth's oceans have a continuous mountain range, called a mid-ocean ridge. These ridges are greater than 80,000 km long in total. The Earth's mid-ocean ridges are located above rising currents in mantle convection cells. You might think that the ridges are formed by the upward push of the rising mantle material, but that's not the reason. The ridges stand high because they are heated by the hot rising material. Like most materials, rocks expand when they are heated.

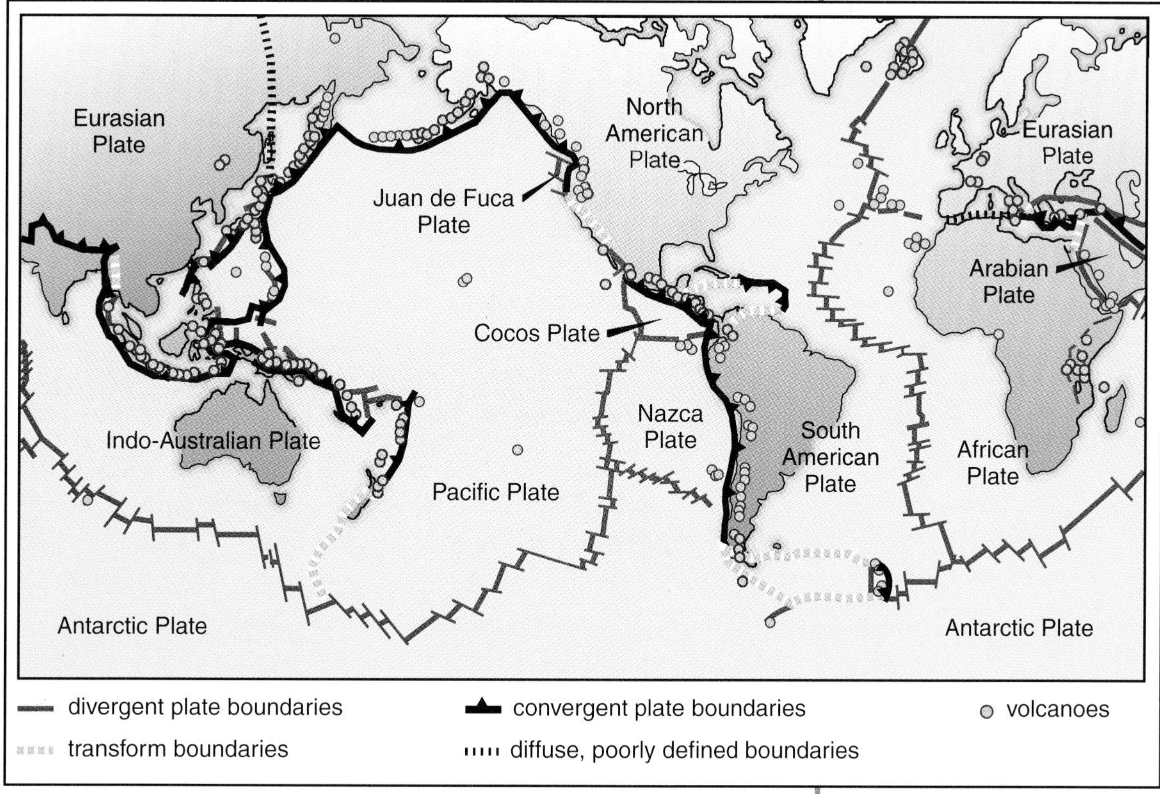

As the hot mantle rock rises up toward the mid-ocean ridge, some of it melts, to form molten rock called magma. The magma is less dense than the surrounding rocks, so it rises up to form volcanoes along the ridge. The reason for the melting is not obvious. As the rock

rises, it stays at about the same temperature, but the pressure on it decreases, because there is less weight of rock above it. It's known, from laboratory experiments, that the melting temperature of most rocks decreases as the pressure decreases. That's why some of the rising rock forms magma.

When the magma reaches the surface of the ridge, it solidifies to form a rock called basalt. That's how new crust is formed in the oceans. As soon as the new crust is formed, it moves away from the crest of the ridge. The movement is partly from the force of the moving mantle below. It is also partly because of the downhill slope of the ridge away from the crest. The movement of new oceanic crust in both directions away from the crest of a mid-ocean ridge is called sea-floor spreading.

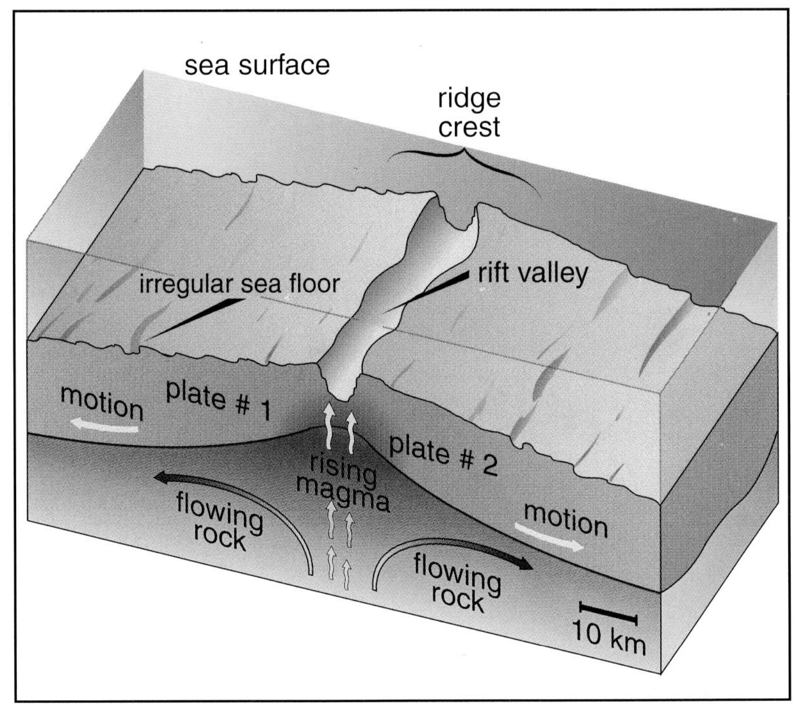

Review and Reflect

Review

1. Think back on the **Key Question:** "Does the rock of the Earth's mantle move?" Answer this question again, based on what you learned in this investigation.
2. Why is the mid-ocean ridge made of volcanic rock?
3. Is the rock that makes up the mid-ocean ridge young or old? Explain your answer.

Reflect

4. Give at least one example of where a convection cell could be formed. Use an example different from any that are presented in this investigation. Describe why the convection occurs.
5. Do you think that a convection cell would be formed in a fluid that is heated at the surface rather than at the bottom? Explain your answer.

Thinking about the Earth System

6. What connections did you discover between convection in the mantle (geosphere) and the oceans (hydrosphere)?
7. How does convection in the Earth's mantle help to shape the geosphere?
8. Describe the flow of energy in the geosphere. Think about the movement of heat energy during mantle convection.

Thinking about Scientific Inquiry

9. a) What hypothesis did you form in this investigation?

   b) Was your hypothesis proven right or wrong by your investigation?

   c) If your hypothesis was wrong, are the results of the investigation still valid? Explain.
10. Explain why a diagram was a good way to show your observations in this investigation.

Investigation 4:

The Movement of the Earth's Lithospheric Plates

Key Question

Before you begin, first think about this key question.

What happens where lithospheric plates meet?

To think about what might happen where plates meet, do these simple demonstrations. Place your hands together palms down, in front of you with your fingers pointing forward and the sides of your thumbs touching. What do you think happens when plates move toward one another? (Push your hands together.) What do you think happens when plates move away from each other? (Move your hands apart.) What might happen when plates slide past one another? (Slide your hands past one another.)

Share your thinking with others in your class. Keep a record of the discussion in your journal.

Materials Needed

For this investigation your group will need:

- scissors
- thick corrugated cardboard
- thin cardboard like a cereal box
- duct tape
- foaming shaving cream
- metric ruler

Investigate

Part A: Modeling Plate Convergence

1. In your group, discuss what you expect would happen when two plates move toward each other. Below are some questions to help your discussion.

Using what you already know about mountains, volcanoes, and earthquakes, work together to find the most reasonable answers to these questions. Record your answers in your journal.

a) How might mountains form there?

b) Might volcanoes develop where plates meet? If so, why?

c) Could there be earthquakes where plates collide? Why?

2. You are now going to model what happens when two plates move toward one another.

With scissors, cut out two pieces of corrugated cardboard. Make each piece about 8 cm wide and about 20 cm long.

Also cut out one piece of cereal-box cardboard, about 8 cm wide and about 15 cm long.

Assemble the pieces of cardboard as shown in the diagram.

When you are ready to run your model, you will be squirting some shaving cream onto the cereal-box cardboard to make a layer about 3 mm thick.

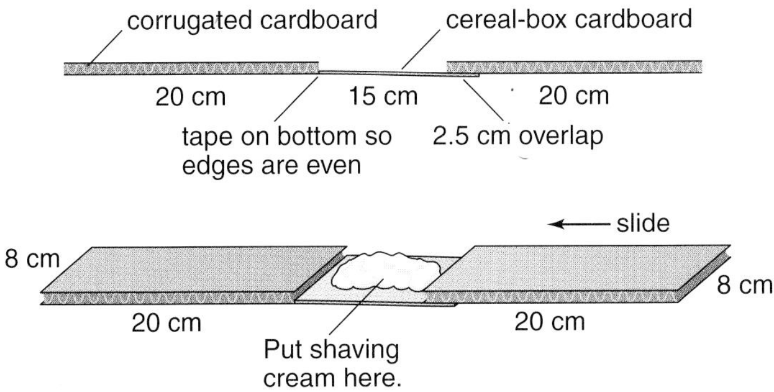

3. You have set up a model of what happens when two plates move toward each other. The process you are modeling is called plate convergence. (The motion of two things toward one another is called convergence.)

The two pieces of corrugated cardboard represent continental plates, and the cereal-box cardboard represents an oceanic plate. The shaving cream represents ocean-floor sediment.

a) Predict what you think will happen when you push the two pieces together until one of the pieces of corrugated cardboard has moved 5 cm beneath the other piece of corrugated cardboard. Also record the reason(s) for your prediction.

b) Draw a side-view diagram of your prediction. On this drawing, use arrows to show the direction of plate movements.

4. Make a data table to record your observations.

   Use this example or design your own.

MEASUREMENTS OF CONVERGENT PLATE MOVEMENT			
Distance plates moved together	**Shape (drawing)**	**Height (cm)**	**Width (cm)**
2.5 cm			
5.0 cm			
7.5 cm			
10.0 cm			
12.5 cm			
15 cm			
17.5 cm			

5. When you are ready, apply the layer of shaving cream, as described in **Step 2** above.

   Now push the two pieces of cardboard together slowly, 2.5 cm at a time. Let the model run until one of the corrugated-cardboard continents has moved under the other corrugated-cardboard continent about 5 cm.

   a) Describe what happens as the pieces of cardboard move toward one another.

   b) In your notebook, make a sketch of what the model looks like after the two continents have collided and the one has moved underneath the other.

   c) How did your results compare to your predictions?

6. Now look at this map, which shows the plate boundaries. The arrows show the direction the plates are moving.

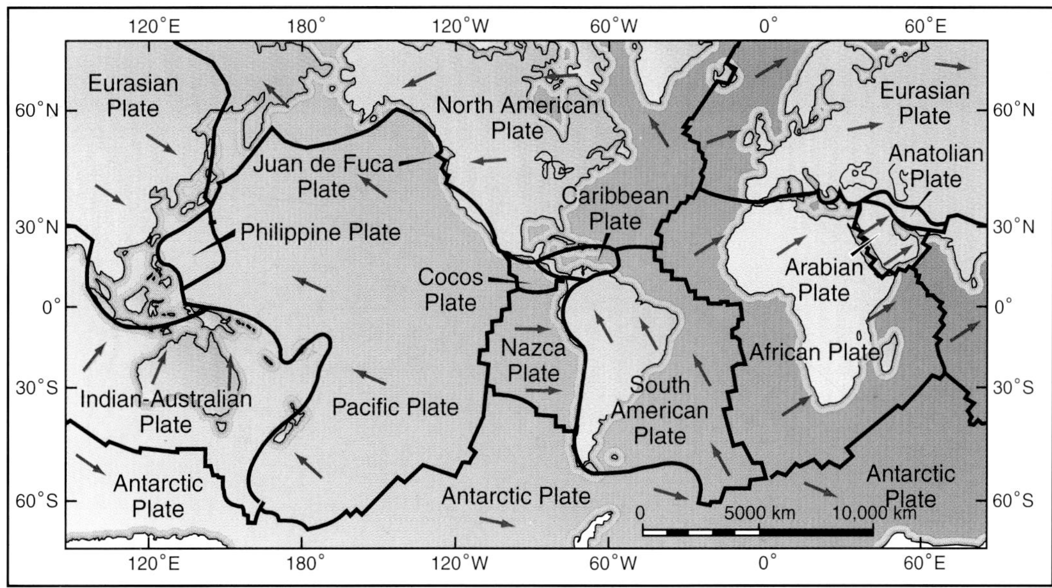

Look closely at those points where an oceanic plate is touching a continental plate. A good example is South America, where the Nazca Plate and the South American Plate are moving toward each other.

a) Where else can you find oceanic plates and continental plates moving toward each other?

b) At a convergent plate boundary, two plates are moving toward each other. How do you think your model might relate to convergent plates like these?

c) What kind of pattern would you expect to see in the locations of earthquakes under the continental plate of South America?

d) Note the places where you think earthquakes or volcanoes might occur.

7. Share your ideas with your group and the rest of the class.

Part B: Modeling Plate Boundaries

1. In **Part A** of this investigation you modeled a convergent plate boundary between continental crust and oceanic crust.

   Read the **Digging Deeper** section that describes other plate boundaries.

   Choose one type of plate boundary to model. You may wish to model a convergent plate boundary between continental and oceanic crust as in **Part A**, using different materials.

   a) Record in your journal the boundary you have decided to model. Write your investigation in the form of a question.

   b) Based on the information you have, predict what you think will happen at the boundary and explain why.

2. In your group discuss the best way to model the boundary you have selected. Consider the materials that are available to you.

   a) List the materials you plan to use. Explain why you chose the materials that you did.

   b) Outline the steps that are required to set up and run your model.

   c) Record all safety factors you need to consider.

3. With the approval of your teacher, demonstrate your model to the class.

Digging  Deeper

The Earth's Lithosphere

In the previous activity you learned that the rock of the Earth's mantle flows slowly in gigantic convection cells. The uppermost part of the mantle, however, does not take part in the convection. That's because its rock is not as hot, and it remains rigid while the rest of the mantle flows. Here's a similar example, on a much smaller scale. If you squeeze Silly Putty® at room temperature, it flows as you squeeze it in your hand. If you cool it in the refrigerator, it stays hard and rigid when you try to squeeze it. In **Investigation 3**, you found that this outermost rigid part of the Earth is called the lithosphere. The thickness of the lithosphere varies from place to place, but mostly it is a hundred or so kilometers. That's still fairly thin, compared to the thickness of the whole mantle, which is about 3000 km. The lithosphere has two parts: the Earth's crust, and the uppermost part of the mantle. The material below the lithosphere is called the asthenosphere ("weak sphere"). Unlike the lithosphere, the asthenosphere does take part in the convection of the mantle. The boundary between the lithosphere and the asthenosphere is really a temperature boundary. Below the boundary the rocks are hot enough to flow. Above the boundary they are cooler and rigid.

In the ocean basins the uppermost part of the lithosphere consists of the basalt that is formed by volcanoes along the mid-ocean ridges. This material is called the oceanic crust. It's only 4 to 8 km thick. The oceanic lithosphere gradually thickens as it moves away from the hot mid-ocean ridge. This is because the temperature boundary where the lithosphere turns into asthenosphere gets deeper in the Earth (see the diagram on the following page).

The Earth's continents form another part of the crust. The continental crust is very different from the oceanic crust.

As You Read...
Think about:

1. ***What is the difference between crust and lithosphere?***
2. ***What is the difference between oceanic crust and continental crust?***
3. ***What is the difference between a subduction zone and a continent–continent collision zone?***
4. ***Why do continents not go down subduction zones?***

It's thicker (mostly 30 to 50 km), its rock is less dense, and it's mostly very much older than the oceanic crust.

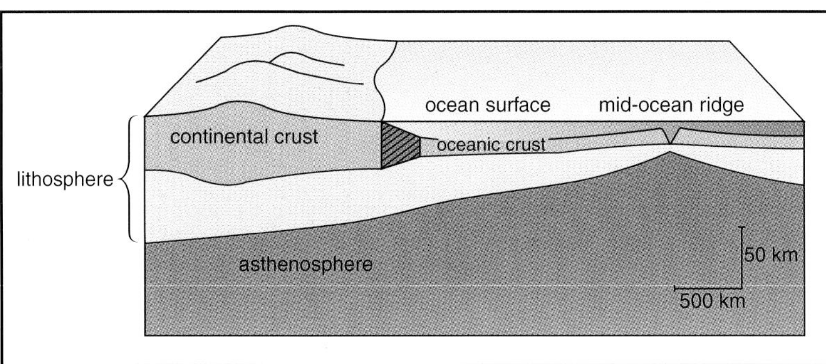

Lithospheric Plates

The lithosphere is not one continuous piece. Instead, it's made up of several very large pieces and a lot of smaller pieces. These pieces are called lithospheric plates (or just plates, for short). They fit together a bit like the pieces of a jigsaw puzzle. The line on the Earth's surface where two plates are in contact with each other is called a plate boundary.

Everywhere on Earth, the plates are in motion relative to one another. Along some boundaries, called divergent boundaries, plates are moving away from each other. Along other boundaries, called convergent boundaries, plates are moving toward one another.

The mid-ocean ridges, which you learned about in the last investigation, are divergent plate boundaries. As the plates move away from each other, new plate material is produced on either side of the ridge.

There is also a third kind of boundary, called a transform boundary, where the plates are moving neither towards one another nor away from one another. Instead, they are simply moving past one another like two cars in different lanes on the highway (only much slower!).

An example of a transform boundary is the San Andreas Fault in California. It appears as a line in the aerial photo to the right. There, the Pacific Plate is moving northwest relative to the North American Plate. Lithosphere is neither created nor destroyed at transform boundaries. For this reason, transform boundaries are sometimes called conservative.

Subduction

Scientists have determined that the surface area of the Earth is not changing over time. Therefore, there must be plate boundaries where plates are consumed, as well as plate boundaries where plates are created. Plate boundaries where one plate dives down underneath another are called subduction zones. The downgoing plate consists of oceanic lithosphere. The other plate, the one that stays at the surface, can also consist of oceanic lithosphere, or it can be a continent. The place where the downgoing plate bends downward is marked by a deep trench on the ocean floor. Earthquakes and volcanoes are very common along subduction zones. The downgoing plate is eventually absorbed into the mantle, but scientists are just beginning to understand how that happens.

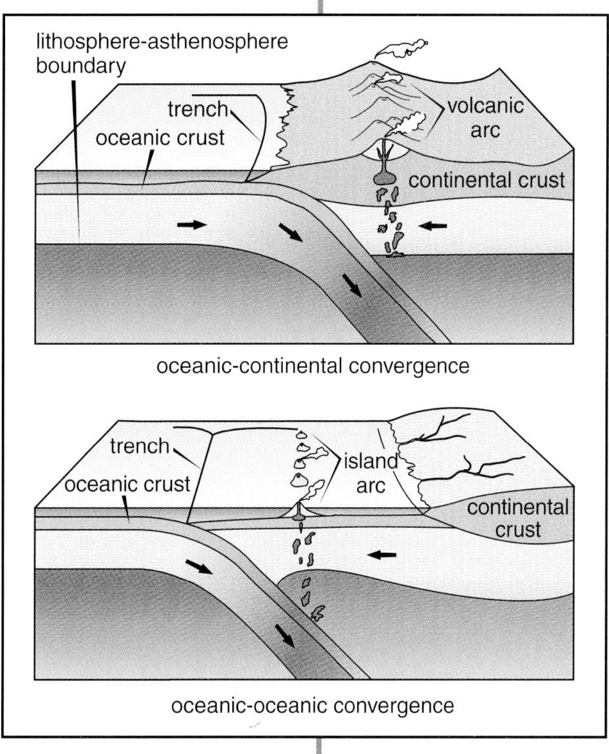

Continent–Continent Collision

Subduction zones can make an ocean basin close up completely. When that happens, two continents meet at the subduction zone. Continents are less dense than the mantle, so they do not go down the subduction zone. It is like pushing a wooden board down into the water: the board tries to float up to the surface again. When the two continents meet, one of the continents is pushed horizontally beneath the other continent. The movement eventually stops, when the force of friction between the continents becomes large enough.

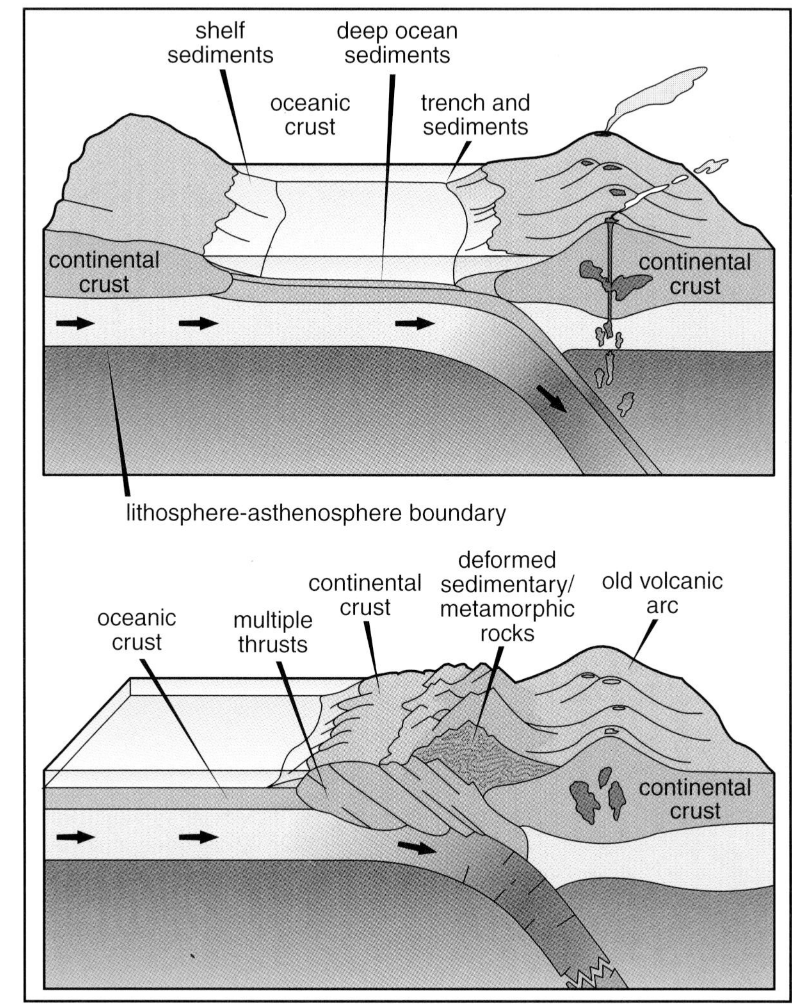

Continent–continent collision zones are places where continents are thickest. Where a continent is thicker, it extends deeper down in the mantle, and its surface stands higher above sea level. There is one place on the Earth today where continent–continent collision is happening: India is slowly being pushed under southern Asia. That collision has produced the Himalayas, which are the highest mountains on Earth, and the Tibetan Plateau, which is the highest large plateau on Earth.

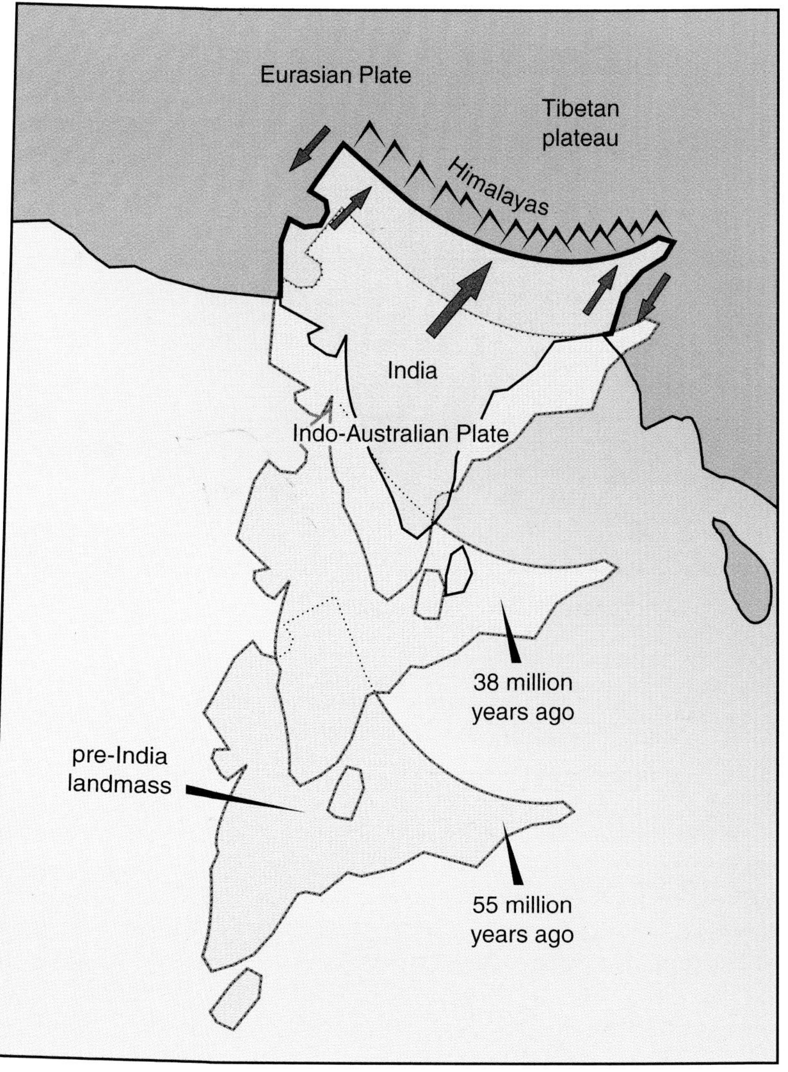

Review and Reflect

Review

1. What types of plate boundaries are found in or along the continental United States?
2. Why are folded mountain ranges found where plates converge? Why are folded mountains uncommon where plates move apart?
3. The Appalachian Mountains in the eastern United States are made up of folded rocks. Do you think that this suggests that this region was once the front edge of colliding plates, spreading plates, or sliding plates? Explain your reasoning.

Reflect

4. Why does the surface of a thicker continent stand higher above sea level than the surface of a thinner continent?
5. Would you expect volcanoes to form where plates slide past one another? Would you expect earthquakes? Explain your answers.

Thinking about the Earth System

6. Movement of the Earth's plates can create and destroy ocean basins. It can change the shape of oceans, the circulation of ocean water, and the depth of water in the ocean. Give an example of how plate tectonics might affect life on land or in the oceans (the biosphere).
7. When an oceanic plate is subducted beneath another plate, some water-rich sediment from the ocean crust descends into the mantle. There is also some water that is trapped within parts of the subducting plate that underlie the sediments. How does this process connect the hydrosphere and the geosphere?

Thinking about Scientific Inquiry

8. Why are models useful in scientific inquiry?
9. What are some problems associated with the use of models?
10. Describe how you used mathematics for science inquiry in this investigation.

Investigation 5:

Earthquakes, Volcanoes, and Mountains

Before you begin, first think about this key question.

How are earthquakes, volcanoes, and mountains related?

In **Investigation 2** you discovered how earthquakes helped shed light on what is inside the Earth. You also found that earthquakes and volcanoes occur along subduction zones. Is that the only place that you find earthquakes and volcanoes? What makes them happen? How are mountains related to earthquakes and volcanoes?

Share your thinking with others in your group and with your class. Keep a record of the discussion in your journal.

Materials Needed

For this investigation your group will need:

- colored pencils (3 different colors)
- copy of a world map

Investigate

1. Discuss the following questions in your group. Be sure to explain your answers. Record the results of your discussion in your journal.

a) Can any mountain have a volcano erupt from it?

b) Do earthquakes and volcanoes always occur in the same area?

c) Do earthquakes and volcanoes always occur at the same time?

2. Look closely at *Table 1*. The data table shows recent earthquakes from around the world. The data was collected at regional seismograph stations.

Discuss the terms used in the table. Describe in your journal what the following terms mean and how they relate to the table.

a) Latitude

b) Longitude

c) Depth

d) Magnitude

Table 1: Subset of Seismograph Station Results for One Week

Latitude	Longitude	Depth (kilometers)	Magnitude (Richter Scale)	Occurrence Region
47°N	151°E	141	5.2	Kuril Islands
28°S	178°W	155	5.0	Kermadec Islands
30°N	52°E	33	4.2	Iran
36°N	140°E	69	4.7	Honshu, Japan
34°N	103°E	33	4.3	Gansu, China
40°S	177°E	27	4.8	New Zealand
0°N	36°E	10	4.6	Kenya, Africa
38°N	21°E	33	4.6	Ionian Sea
16°N	47°W	10	4.7	N. Mid-Atlantic Ridge
6°S	147°E	100	4.4	New Guinea
55°N	164°W	150	4.5	Unimak Island, Alaska
24°S	67°W	176	4.1	Argentina
13°N	91°W	33	4.2	Guatemala coast
4°N	76°W	171	5.6	Colombia
40°N	125°W	2	4.5	N. California coast
5°S	102°E	33	4.4	S. Sumatra, Indonesia
44°S	16°W	10	4.6	S. Mid-Atlantic Ridge
51°N	179°E	33	4.4	Aleutian Islands
15°S	71°W	150	4.2	Peru
49°N	128°W	10	4.7	Vancouver, Canada
35°N	103°E	33	4.3	Gansu, China

3. Use a copy of the world map shown.

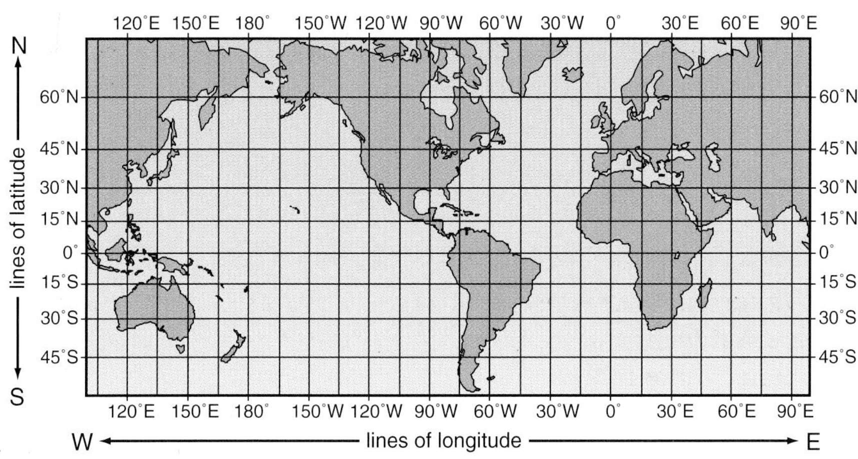

a) Plot the locations of recent earthquakes shown in *Table 1*, using a colored dot for each earthquake.

b) Make a key at the bottom of the map to show what the dot represents.

4. Use your copy of the map with the earthquakes plotted.

a) Plot the locations of recent volcanoes shown in *Table 2* on the next page. Use a different color and symbol than you did when plotting earthquakes.

b) Make sure your key reflects this new information.

Table 2: Global Volcanic Activity Over One-Month Period			
Latitude	**Longitude**	**Location**	**Region**
1°S	29°E	Nyamuragira	Congo, Eastern Africa
38°N	15°E	Stromboli	Aeolian Islands, Italy
37°N	15°E	Etna	Sicily, Italy
15°S	71°W	Sabancaya	Peru
0°	78°W	Guagua Pichincha	Ecuador
12°N	87°W	San Cristobal	Nicaragua
0°	91°W	Cerro Azul	Galapagos, Ecuador
19°N	103°W	Colima	Western Mexico
19°N	155°W	Kilauea	Hawaii, USA
56°N	161°E	Shiveluch	Kamchatka, Russia
54°N	159°E	Karymsky	Kamchatka, Russia
43°N	144°E	Akan	Hokkaido, Japan
39°N	141°E	Iwate	Honshu, Japan
42°N	140°E	Komaga-take	Hokkaido, Japan
1°S	101°E	Kerinci	Sumatra, Indonesia
4°S	145°E	Manam	Papua, New Guinea
5°S	148°E	Langila	Papua, New Guinea
15°S	167°E	Aoba	Vanuatu
16°N	62°W	Soufriere Hills	Montserrat, West Indies
12°N	86°W	Masaya	Nicaragua
37°N	25°W	Sete Cidades	Azores

Inquiry

Using Maps and Data Tables as Scientific Tools

Scientists collect and review data using tools. You may think of tools as only physical objects such as shovels and hand lenses, but forms in which information is gathered, stored, and presented are also tools for scientists. In this investigation you are using scientific tools: data tables and maps.

5. Use your map to answer the following questions:
   a) List several locations where an earthquake happened close to a volcanic eruption.
   b) List several locations where an earthquake happened far from the nearest volcanic eruption.
   c) Describe any pattern or patterns in the locations of earthquakes and volcanoes.
   d) How might additional data help you to find patterns, trends, and relationships between volcanoes and earthquakes?
6. The next map shows the major mountain chains of the world.

a) Add this information to your map. Use a different color and a symbol to represent the mountains.

b) Make sure your key reflects this new information.

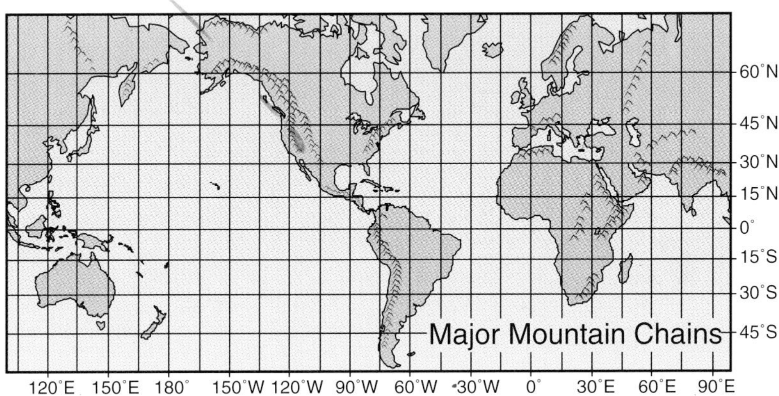

7. You now have a map showing the correlation between earthquakes, volcanoes, and major mountain chains in the world. Compare your map to the map of plate boundaries on P27. Discuss and record your ideas about the following. Share your observations and discuss your ideas with the rest of the class.

   a) List three places where earthquakes, volcanoes, and mountains occur together.

   b) List three volcanic mountain chains.

   c) Explain the relationship you think there is among earthquakes, volcanoes, and mountains.

8. The *IES* web site lists several eathquakes and volcanoes. Each group should choose one volcano and one earthquake to investigate. You may wish to divide this task so that each group takes responsibility for a different information source. These might include:

   - Earth science textbooks and reference books.
   - Encyclopedias.
   - CD-ROMs.
   - The *IES* web site at www.agiweb.org/ies.

   Work together to use what you've learned about plate tectonics to explain why these earthquakes and volcanoes occurred. Discuss your findings with the rest of the class.

   a) Record the results of your discussions in your journal.

Inquiry

Correlations as Evidence

A correlation is a relationship or connection between two or more things. Correlations are often the first kind of evidence gathered when trying to explain an occurrence.

Digging  Deeper

As You Read...
Think about:

1. *What is the cause of earthquakes?*
2. *How are faults and earthquakes related?*
3. *What is the cause of volcanoes?*
4. *How does gas content affect how a volcano erupts?*
5. *How is volcanism at a hotspot different from volcanism at a mid-ocean ridge. How are they similar?*
6. *Why are mountains found in regions where the lithosphere is thick?*

EARTHQUAKES, VOLCANOES, AND MOUNTAINS

The Nature of Earthquakes

Like all solids, rocks have strength. It takes a large force to break them. Plate movements cause large forces to build up within the lithosphere, and at certain times and places, the forces become greater than the strength of the rock. The rock then breaks, along a fracture surface that sometimes extend for tens of kilometers. This surface is called a fault. Faults are fractures in the Earth's surface along which there has been rupture and movement in the past. When the rocks break, the rocks on either side of the fracture plane slide past one another, until the forces are relieved. Strong vibrations are produced as the rock masses slide past one another. Those vibrations are felt as an earthquake. The vibrations travel away in all directions in the form of seismic waves, which you learned about earlier. Over time, the fracture "heals," making the strength of the rock greater again. For this reason, faults tend to slip, then stick, then slip again, and so on. As the rocks on either side of a fault slide past one another, they produce strong vibrations.

Earthquakes and Plate Movements

Many of the largest earthquakes occur along subduction zones, as the downgoing plate slides downward. The pattern of forces within the plate that cause the earthquake fracture is very complicated. The result of those forces, however, is the occurrence

of earthquakes that range from very shallow to as deep as hundreds of kilometers. Earthquakes are also very common in continent–continent collision zones, as one continent is pushed beneath another.

Along transform boundaries, the two plates slide parallel to one another along a surface called a transform fault. If the fault becomes locked for a long period of time and then suddenly slips, a major earthquake results. Along some transform boundaries, however, the fault slips continuously, causing nothing more than very minor earthquakes. The San Andreas Fault, in California, is an unusually long transform fault. It is locked in southern California, in the vicinity of Los Angeles. It is also locked in central California, in the vicinity of San Francisco. That is why the earthquake hazard is great in both of those cities.

The Nature of Volcanoes

A volcano is a place where molten rock, and also solid volcanic fragments and volcanic gases, are erupted at the Earth's surface. At certain times and places, rock deep in the Earth is melted, to form magma. The magma rises upward, because it is less dense than the surrounding rock. It does not always reach the surface before it crystallizes to rock again, but when it does, it forms a volcano.

Volcanoes vary a lot in how they erupt. The most important factor is the gas content of the magma. All magmas have gases dissolved in them, in the same way that soft drinks have carbon dioxide dissolved in them to make them fizzy. As the magma gets close to the surface, the pressure on the magma decreases. That causes some of the gas to bubble out of the magma. Magma with low gas content comes out of the volcano without violent explosions and then flows peacefully down the sides of the volcano. Magmas with high gas content cause powerful explosions when they approach the surface.

The explosions blow globs of magma and pieces of broken rock high into the atmosphere. Large explosive volcanic eruptions are the most serious hazard humankind faces, except for extremely rare impacts of large meteorites.

Volcanoes and Plate Movements

In **Investigation 3** you learned how volcanoes are formed along mid-ocean ridges. Those volcanoes are very numerous, but most of them are deep in the ocean. In some places, however, volcanic activity on a mid-ocean ridge is strong enough to build an island above sea level. Iceland is a good example of that.

Most large volcanoes occur along subduction zones. Certain scientists think that some volcanoes near subduction zones are caused when parts of the subducting ocean crust reach a certain depth and begin to melt. Many scientists, however, believe that the cause of most subduction zone volcanoes has to do with the water that is contained in the rocks of the ocean crust. At a certain depth down the subduction zone, the water is released from the rocks. The water rises up into the mantle above the subducted plate. Laboratory experiments have shown that adding water lowers the melting point of the mantle rocks. Whichever way the magma is generated, it rises up to feed volcanoes along the subduction zone.

There is another kind of volcano called a hot spot volcano. It is caused by a hot spot in the mantle that generates magma for long periods of time. Scientists think that hot spots don't move, and so a line of volcanoes forms as the plate moves over the hot spot. The orientation of that line and ages of the volcanoes that make it up reveal the direction and speed of plate movement. Unlike most other volcanoes, hot spot volcanoes can occur far from plate boundaries. The Hawaiian Islands and Yellowstone Park are good examples of hot spot volcanism.

The Association of Earthquakes and Volcanoes

Along subduction zones, major earthquakes and large volcanoes are both common. Most of the Pacific Ocean is rimmed with subduction zones. That's why earthquakes and volcanoes are so common in countries that border the Pacific. You might have heard that the Pacific Rim is called the "Ring of Fire." In continent–continent collision zones, as in southern Asia, earthquakes are common but volcanoes are not formed. Countries like China, India, Iran, and Turkey experience major earthquakes but not volcanoes.

Mountain Building

Most of the world's large mountain ranges are formed where two lithospheric plates collide. Where two plates converge at a subduction zone, enormous volumes of material are added to the region. Some of this material is sediment that is scraped off from the downgoing plate. Also, magma from deep in the subduction zone rises up to feed volcanoes on the plate that isn't subducting. Some of the magma stays below the surface to form deep igneous rocks. As the crust near the subduction zone grows in volume, its base becomes lower and its top becomes higher. It's very much like a block of wood floating in water: the thicker the block, the lower its base, and the higher its top. The rocks of the Earth's lithosphere float on the denser mantle below, so when the lithosphere becomes thicker, mountains are formed. The Andes, along the west coast of South America, have been formed in that way. The same thing happens when two continents collide. As one of the continents is shoved beneath the other, the lithosphere becomes thicker, so it rises up to form a mountain range. The Himalayas, in southern Asia, have been formed in that way.

Review and Reflect

Review

1. Review your answers to **Investigate, Step 1**. Answer the questions again, using what you learned in this investigation. Be sure to explain your answers.
   a) Can any mountain have a volcano erupt from it?
   b) Do earthquakes and volcanoes always occur in the same area?
   c) Do earthquakes and volcanoes always occur at the same time?
2. Where do most earthquakes occur in the United States? Why?
3. Where in the United States are most volcanoes found? Why?

Reflect

4. How does the gas content of a magma affect the shape of a volcano?
5. Dynamic means powerful or active. How has this investigation added to your understanding of Earth as a dynamic planet?

Thinking about the Earth System

6. How does the hydrosphere influence the nature of volcanic eruptions?
7. How do volcanic eruptions affect the atmosphere?
8. How are volcanoes, earthquakes, and mountains (geosphere) linked to the biosphere?

   Remember to write in any connections that you have made between volcanoes, earthquakes, mountains, and the Earth System on your *Earth System Connection* sheet.

Thinking about Scientific Inquiry

9. When did you form your hypotheses in this investigation?
10. What scientific tools did you use in this investigation?

Investigation 6:

Earth's Moving Continents

Key Question

Before you begin, first think about this key question.

Have the continents and oceans always been in the positions they are today?

In **Investigation 4** you learned that the Earth's lithospheric plates move relative to one another. Do they go anywhere? How far do they move? Have they always been moving? Have there always been the same number of plates?

Share your thinking with others in your class. Keep a record of the discussion in your journal.

Materials Needed

For this investigation your group will need:

- a copy of the world map cutout showing the continents and the continental shelf
- scissors
- construction paper
- glue

Investigate

1. Look at the map of the world on the following page, centered on the Atlantic Ocean. Look especially at the edges of the African and South American continents.

The dashed lines show the continental shelf, a shallow platform along the edge of all the continents.

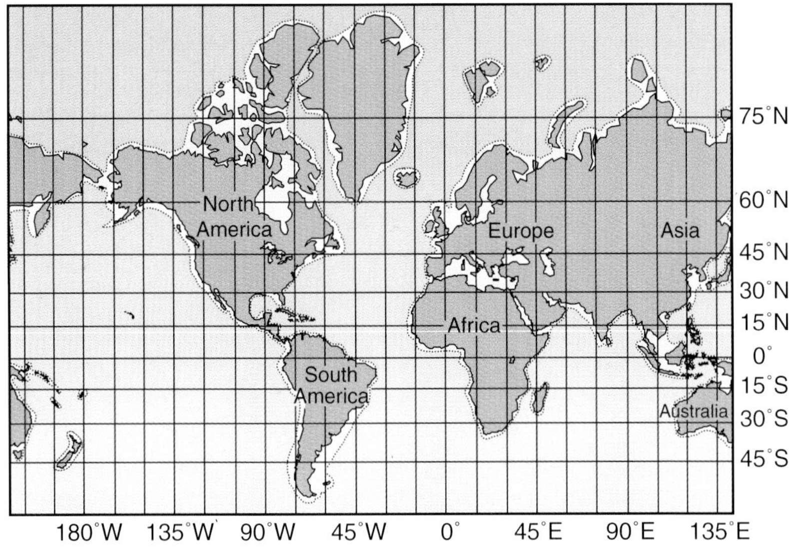

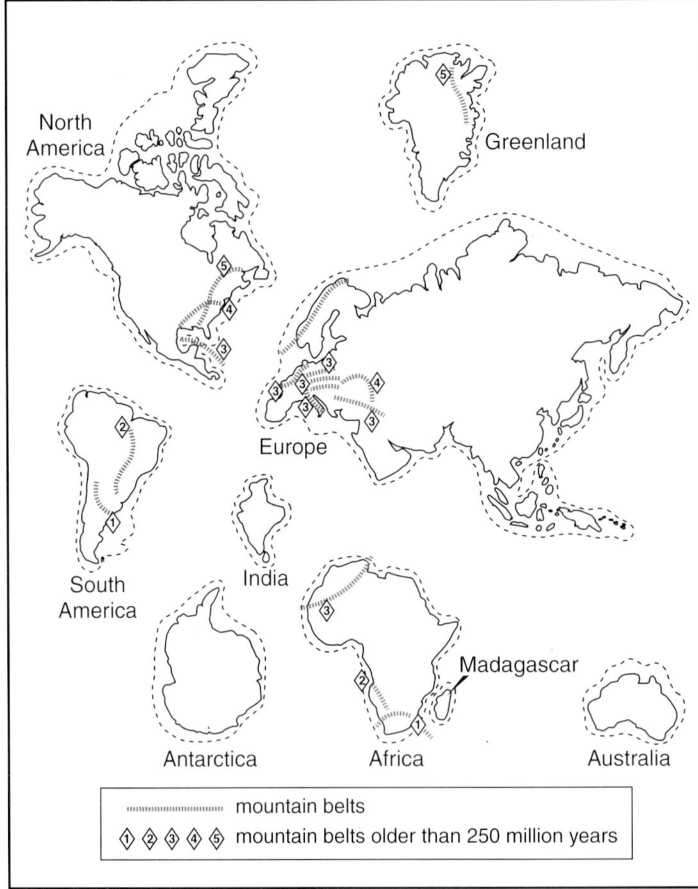

a) Describe the match between the East Coast of South America and the West Coast of Africa.

b) Describe the match between the bulge of West Africa and the outline of the East Coast of North America.

2. Examine the figure to the left that has all of the continents separated from one another so that they can be cut out with a pair of scissors.

Get a copy of this map. Use scissors to cut out the continents along the outer edges of the continental shelves, along the dashed lines.

3. Use the cutouts of the continents like pieces of a jigsaw puzzle.

   On a sheet of construction paper, try to arrange the continents as one large landmass.

   a) Describe the locations of any overlapping areas.

   b) How confident are you that the continents were linked together at some time in the past?

4. Several of the world's mountain ranges that appear on a continent today are similar in age and form to mountain ranges that today are on another continent. Some of these mountain ranges are shown in the continent cutouts. They are numbered according to those that have similarities with one another.

   a) Do the mountain ranges with common features line up with one another in your arrangement of the continents?

b) Does this information give supporting evidence for your arrangement of the continents, or does it argue against your arrangement of the continents?

c) Make changes in your model in light of the evidence you have.

5. Several fossils are found on particular landmasses but not on others. Review the following evidence:

Cynognathus was a reptile that lived in what are now Brazil and Africa.

Lystrosaurus was found in Central Africa, India, and Antarctica.

Megosaurus was found in the southern tip of South America and the southern tip of Africa

Glossopteris was a fern found in Antarctica, Australia, India, southern Africa, and southern South America

The map shows the locations of the fossils.

Inquiry

Using Evidence Collected by Others

In this investigation you are using evidence that you have been provided to formulate your ideas about how the continents may have fit together. Scientists must often rely on evidence gathered by others to develop their hypotheses.

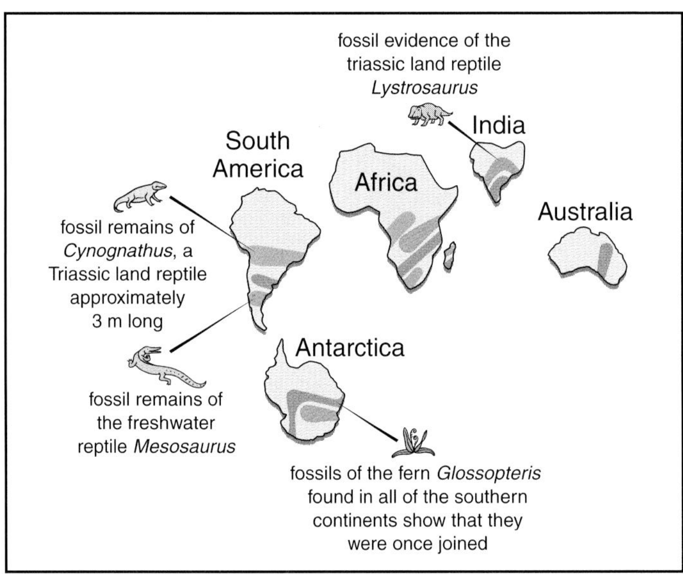

a) Add this information to the landmasses you are arranging on your construction paper.

b) Does this new information strengthen or weaken your model? Explain.

c) Make changes in your model in light of the new evidence you have.

d) What new information might change your model?

6. Evidence produced by glaciers from long ago provides geoscientists with ideas about the movement of continents. Imagine a bulldozer plowing a pile of soil, then stopping, backing up, and driving away. Like a bulldozer, a glacier plows a large pile of rock and sediment. When the glacier melts, the "plowed" deposit, called a terminal moraine, is left at the front of the glacier.

   Examine the next map, which shows where evidence of ice sheets 300 million years old has been found in the Southern Hemisphere. The red line on the map connects all the places where terminal moraines from this time have been found on the continents, and the arrows show the direction of glacier movement.

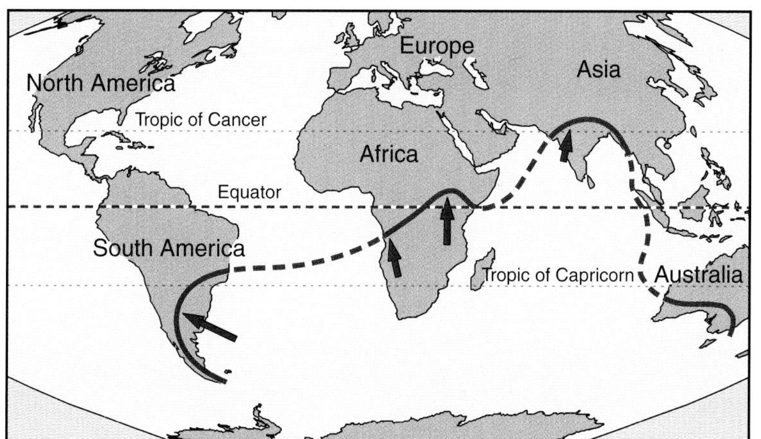

   a) Add the information to your tracing-paper landmasses, including the extent of glacial ice and the direction of its movement.

   b) How do you think this evidence might support the idea that these continents were once joined together?

   c) Make changes in your model in light of the new evidence you have.

7. When you are satisfied with the model you have created, glue your landmasses onto the construction paper. Include a key or legend for all the information you have added.

   a) What additional new information would you need in order to improve the model?

8. Share your model with the class. Discuss the evidence behind the model.

Inquiry

Sharing Findings

An important part of a scientific experiment is sharing the results with others. Scientists do this whenever they think that they have discovered scientifically interesting information. In this investigation you are sharing your ideas with other groups.

Digging  Deeper

As You Read...
Think about:
1. ***In your own words, explain the theory of continental drift.***
2. ***What was Pangea?***
3. ***How is a suture zone formed?***
4. ***Why is the Pacific Ocean shrinking?***

SUPERCONTINENTS

Continental Drift

When you tried to assemble the continents like jigsaw-puzzle pieces, it probably seemed natural to you that Africa and South America fit together fairly well if you remove the ocean. This is one of the pieces of evidence that caused scientists 100 years ago to think that the two continents were once a single continent. The idea is that the single continent broke apart and the pieces drifted away from each other, to form the Atlantic Ocean. The fit of the continents is not the only evidence that supports the theory of continental drift. For example, you saw in your investigation that fossils of the same plants and animals are found in areas that are now separated by wide oceans and are in very different climatic zones.

Does it surprise you that it took a long time for most geoscientists to accept the theory of continental drift, even with the good evidence you worked with? The main reason was that no one could think of a way that the continents could plow along through the mantle beneath. When the theory of plate tectonics was developed in the 1960s, however, it gave a natural explanation for continental drift. Plate tectonic theory proposes that the outermost layer of the Earth, the lithosphere, behaves as a rigid layer. The lithosphere is broken into plates. These plates move relative to one another at their boundaries. Nowadays nearly all geoscientists believe in the reality of continental drift.

Supercontinents

In **Investigation 4** you learned that subduction can lead to the closing of an ocean and then continent–continent collision. When that happens, two separate continents

become one large continent. Geoscientists are now sure that about 250 million years ago all of the Earth's continents were gathered into a single very large "supercontinent." That happened by a long series of continent–continent collisions. That supercontinent has been named Pangea (***pan*** means "all", and ***gea*** means "land"). The diagram below is a map that shows geoscientists' best estimate of what Pangea looked like.

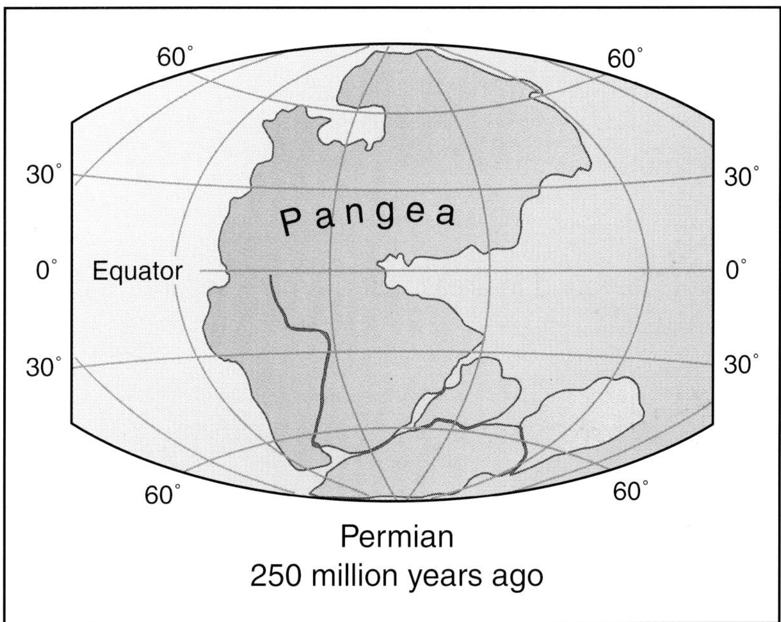

Permian
250 million years ago

You've already learned about some of the evidence for the existence of Pangea: for example, the fit of continents like Africa and South America, and similar fossils that are now far apart but must have been together in the past. Another important kind of evidence is the existence of former continent–continent collision zones, called suture zones, in the interiors of today's continents. These suture zones are the places where the earlier continents came together to form Pangea. The Appalachian Mountains, in eastern North America, are an example of these suture zones.

The Breakup of Pangea

About 200 million years ago the pattern of convection cells in the mantle changed, for reasons geoscientists are not yet sure about. This change caused Pangea to slowly split apart into several pieces. This process is called continental rifting. The pieces, which we know as today's continents, gradually drifted apart. That caused the Atlantic Ocean and the Indian Ocean, and the Antarctic Ocean to grow larger. The rifts didn't develop in exactly the same places where Pangea

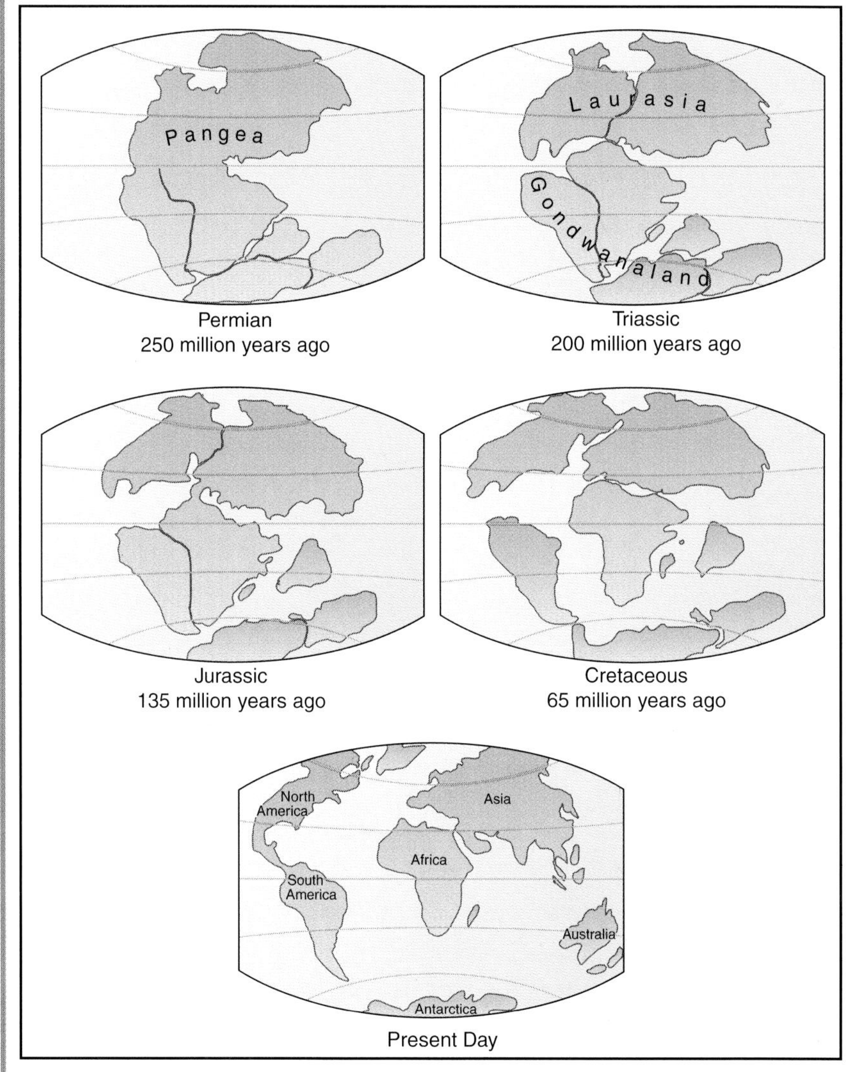

Permian
250 million years ago

Triassic
200 million years ago

Jurassic
135 million years ago

Cretaceous
65 million years ago

Present Day

was first sutured together. For example, the rift that formed the Atlantic Ocean was located to the east of the present Appalachian Mountains. That's why you sometimes hear that areas along the East Coast of the United States were once part of Africa! What does that really mean? They were on the ***east*** side of the ocean that vanished when northern Africa and North America were sutured together, but they were left on the ***west*** side of the new Atlantic Ocean that formed when Pangea was rifted apart.

There's evidence of earlier supercontinents, much farther back in geologic time. There seems to have been a supercontinent that formed and then rifted apart about 600 million years ago. Not nearly as much is known about the nature of that earlier supercontinent, because of the later movement of the continents while Pangea was being assembled.

At the time of Pangea, the Pacific Ocean was the world's only ocean! As the new oceans (the Atlantic, Indian, and Antarctic Oceans) have widened after Pangea was rifted apart, the Pacific Ocean has shrunk, although it's still the largest ocean. As you saw in **Investigation 4**, today's Pacific Ocean is surrounded by subduction zones. Those are the places where the floor of the Pacific Ocean is being consumed. What's going to happen in the geologic future? Will the Pacific continue to shrink, until all of today's continents collect there to form a new supercontinent? Or will the Pacific expand again, and the new oceans close up again to form a supercontinent where Pangea once existed? Most geoscientists think that the latter will happen.

Today scientists can actually measure how the plates are moving. They use orbiting satellites to directly measure the plates' movements as they happen. Only since the development of the satellite-based global positioning system (GPS) has this direct measurement of continental drift been possible.

Review and Reflect

Review

1. Look again at the **Key Question** for this investigation: "Have the continents and oceans always been in the positions they are today?" In your journal, write down what you have learned from your investigations that provides an answer.
2. What kinds of evidence can be used to identify the former existence of a supercontinent?
3. In your own words, explain the theory of continental drift.

Reflect

4. Why do you think it took so long for most geoscientists to accept the theory of continental drift?
5. What additional evidence would you like to have to prove that the Earth's surface has moved and is moving?
6. What additional questions would you like to be answered and explained?

Thinking about the Earth System

7. What connections has your investigation revealed about the dynamic planet and the geosphere?
8. What links to the biosphere did you make in this investigation?
9. How was the hydrosphere connected to the evidence that you used?

   Don't forget to write any connections you uncover on the *Earth System Connection* sheet.

Thinking about Scientific Inquiry

10. How did you use evidence to develop scientific ideas?
11. How did you communicate your findings to others in a way that could be seen and understood?

Investigation 7:

Natural Hazards and Our Dynamic Planet

Putting It All Together

Key Question

Before you begin this final investigation, first think about this key question.

What natural hazards do dynamic events cause?

Think about the movement of Earth's lithospheric plates. What hazards can they pose to humans? Think about all you have learned in the previous investigations. Share your thinking with others in your class. Keep a record of the discussion in your journal.

Materials Needed

For this investigation, each group may need:

- reference materials
- access to computer word processing and desktop publishing (if possible)
- range of general craft materials required to make a brochure

Investigate

1. Consider what might happen if an earthquake or volcanic eruption occurred in or close to a community. In your group, brainstorm the ideas that you have about the questions below:

a) What would happen to local dams, reservoirs, or water supply stations?

b) What would happen to schools, homes, and government buildings?

c) What would happen to electrical power plants?

d) What would happen to local hospitals?

2. Share your ideas in a class discussion.

   Do not be too concerned at this point whether or not your initial ideas are correct. Just ensure that all ideas are given. The goal of this investigation is to learn about natural hazards. Pay careful attention to what your classmates contribute to this discussion.

3. Here are just some of the hazards that can be caused by volcanoes and earthquakes.

Event	Effect	Examples
Volcanoes	Eruption with lava flow	• lava streams burn all in their path
	Eruption with ash fall	• aircraft endangered, roofs collapse
	Lahar (mud flow)	• Large, fast-moving river of mud
	Pyroclastic flow	• hot mobile flow of volcanic material
	Lateral blast	• explosive wave knocks down all in its path
	Volcano collapses	• land drops away—homes threatened
	Volcanic gases	• volcanic pollution
Earthquakes	Ground motion	• buildings and bridges collapse
	Fault displacement	• roads crack, rail tracks split
	Fires	• ruptures in gas lines cause building fires
	Landslides	• shaking causes rock to slide downhill
	Liquefaction	• ground becomes like quicksand
	Failures of dams	• flooding

4. Using the resources available in your class, school media center, public library, and home, select one of the terms to research. Find out:
   - what the hazard is;
   - how it forms and works;
   - how it affects living and non-living things;
   - what steps citizens can take to prepare for such hazards;
   - what people can do to protect themselves once the hazard starts;
   - where people can get further information.

Here are some of the factors you could consider when assessing potential earthquake hazards for a particular area, or designing an investigation into earthquake hazards:

- closeness to active earthquake faults;
- seismic history of the region (how often earthquakes occur; time since last earthquake);
- building construction (type of building and foundation; architectural layout; materials used; quality of workmanship; extent to which earthquake resistance was considered by the designer);
- local conditions (type and condition of soil; slope of the land; fill material; geologic structure of the earth beneath; annual rainfall).

Inquiry

Dividing Tasks

This investigation provides you with an opportunity to mirror the teamwork that often happens in scientific studies. Different scientists often take on responsibility for different parts of a study.

Presenting Information

Scientists are often asked to provide information to the public. In doing so, they need to consider both the message they want to communicate and the persons or groups that will be using the information. Once they are clear about the message and the audience, they can then decide on the best method of presenting the information. These are decisions you also will need to make in this investigation.

Here are some of the factors you could consider when assessing potential volcanic hazards for a particular area:

- volcanic history of the area (how often eruptions occur; time since last eruption?);
- population of the area around the volcano (are there towns and villages in high risk areas?);
- prevailing wind directions (where will most of the volcanic ash settle?);
- topography of the land (where are there valleys and ridges that will direct where the lava and hot gasses flow out of the volcano?).

5. It is important that you find out all you can about your chosen hazard.

   To do this, you may want to divide up the tasks, with each member of your group specializing in a particular aspect, using all information sources available.

   a) List the responsibilities of each group member in your journal.

6. When you are sure you have organized your research in a reasonable way, begin your investigation.

   When each person has conducted his or her research, share and discuss your findings in your group.

   You may think that you need to experiment further, to establish clearly how your hazard works. If necessary, design and model your hazard, using readily available materials.

7. Once you have assembled all the information you need, and completed any tests you think necessary, design a brochure.

   The job of the brochure is to provide information to residents of a community that is close to a potential earthquake or volcano hazard site. Be sure the brochure addresses all the points in **Step 4.**

   Discuss the best way to organize your information to cover these points.

   Here are a number of ideas to consider when designing your brochure:

   - the shape and size of the brochure;

- the color of the paper or card that can be used;
- computer programs that have templates for brochure design;
- artwork, diagrams, charts, or drawings that you can use or create;
- the various talents members of your group have.

Keep in mind that the brochure has size limits and that you may need to find creative ways to include all the information you think is essential.

Work together to produce the best brochure you can, keeping in mind the audience for which it is intended.

8. When all group's brochures are complete, arrange a session where groups look at each brochure in turn.

Digging  **Deeper**

EARTHQUAKE HAZARDS

Earthquakes happen when there is sudden movement of two rock masses along a fracture plane called a fault. Because of large-scale movements of the Earth's lithospheric plates, great forces can build up in rocks. Eventually, when the forces become greater than the strength of the rocks, long fractures form, and the rocks on either side of the fracture surface shift relative to one another. This motion is jerky and irregular, which causes strong vibrations. The vibrations travel away from the fault in the form of seismic waves. Above the fault, the vibrations cause up-and-down motions and side-to-side motions of the ground surface. Those motions are what you feel as an earthquake. Earthquakes vary greatly in their strength. Most earthquakes are so small that they can be detected only with special instruments. Some earthquakes, however, release an enormous amount of energy. They can cause ground motions so strong that people who are out in the open can't even stand up!

As You Read...
Think about:

1. ***What causes earthquakes?***
2. ***What effects can earthquakes have on buildings?***
3. ***What is the hazard associated with liquefaction?***
4. ***What is the difference between an ash fall and an ash flow?***
5. ***What warning signs make volcanic eruptions easier to predict than earthquakes?***

The most serious hazard associated with earthquakes is the collapse of buildings. If a large building is not carefully designed to withstand the shaking of an earthquake, the floors can collapse upon one another in a kind of "pancaking." If the foundation of a building is not adequate, the building can tip over sideways during a strong earthquake. Structural engineers continue to make careful studies on how to design buildings to withstand earthquakes. Cities in areas of the United States that are prone to earthquakes have building codes that builders are required to follow. Loss of life in earthquakes in the United States is much less than in some other countries where buildings are not designed to withstand large earthquakes.

Earthquakes can cause many other kinds of serious damage. In areas with steep land slopes, earthquakes can trigger large and fast-moving landslides. Water mains can be broken, making it difficult to fight fires, which are often caused by earthquakes. In areas where the soil is porous and saturated with water, the earthquake vibrations sometimes cause the material to settle into closer packing of the soil particles. When that happens, the soil can flow like a liquid. The process is called liquefaction. Liquefaction can cause buildings to sink into the ground!

Volcano Hazards

Lava flows from volcanoes are not especially hazardous to human life, because they flow slowly enough for people to get out of their way. Of course, they burn buildings that are in their path! Explosive volcanoes are far more dangerous. Such volcanoes throw enormous quantities of rock and mineral particles, called volcanic ash, high into the atmosphere. The ash settles back to the ground for distances of tens to hundreds of miles. The ash fall forms a blanket as thick as several meters on the ground surface. Even a thin blanket of ash can collapse roofs and kill crops. By far the worst hazard associated with explosive volcanoes, however, is an ash flow. Sometimes, volcanoes erupt ash in such large quantities that it collapses back downward over the volcano and rushes down the slopes of the volcano as a thick mixture of hot ash and volcanic gases. Ash flows move at express-train speeds of hundreds of meters per second. They can travel for tens or hundreds of miles, killing and burying everything in their path.

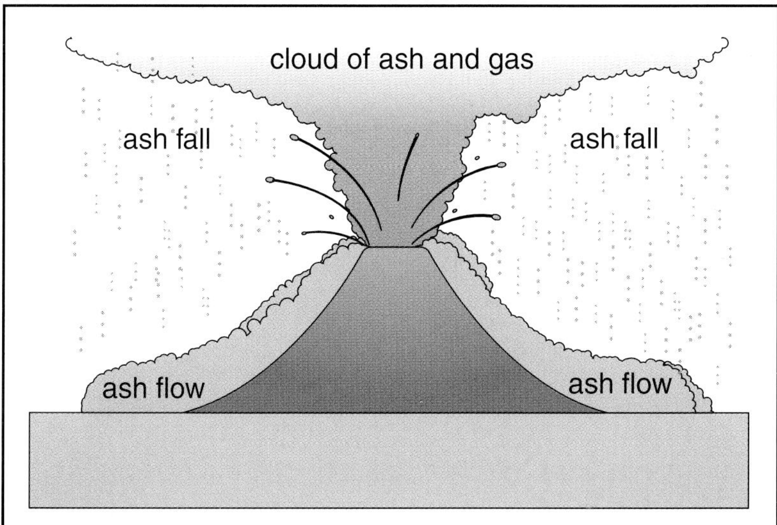

Predicting Earthquakes and Volcanoes

Many attempts have been made to develop ways of predicting earthquakes. So far, no reliable method has been developed. Geoscientists are not sure whether they will ever be successful in predicting earthquakes with a high degree of certainty. If a weather forecast of a major snowstorm is wrong, and it rains instead, that's not a big problem. If there is a forecast of a major earthquake, large numbers of people might be evacuated from a city. If the earthquake didn't happen, think of all the unnecessary economic disruption there would be.

Volcanic eruptions are easier to predict, because most volcanoes give warnings of an eruption. Gases begin to escape from around the volcano. Minor earthquakes in the area beneath the volcano become much more common. Often, the surface of the volcano swells upward enough to be measured by surveying methods. At that point, a major eruption is likely, although not certain. Evacuations based on such observations have saved many lives.

Review and Reflect

Review

1. Describe an example of an earthquake hazard.
2. Describe an example of a volcanic hazard.
3. How do ash falls and ash flows from volcanic eruptions pose hazards to humans?

Reflect

4. What are the advantages and disadvantages of attempting to predict earthquakes and volcanoes?
5. The movement along a fault that causes an earthquake can also damage gas lines and water lines. Why does this pose a problem after an earthquake?
6. Why do you think people live in regions that are prone to volcanic eruptions and earthquakes?
7. Why is the kind of information that you provided for your report useful to the public?

Thinking about the Earth System

8. How might a volcanic eruption affect the biosphere, hydrosphere, or atmosphere in a negative way?
9. How do volcanic eruptions benefit the biosphere, hydrosphere, or atmosphere?

Thinking about Scientific Inquiry

10. Why do scientists present their findings to others?
11. What are some of the advantages to doing scientific work as a team?
12. What inquiry processes did you use in this final investigation? Name at least three processes, where you used them, and how they helped you complete this assignment.

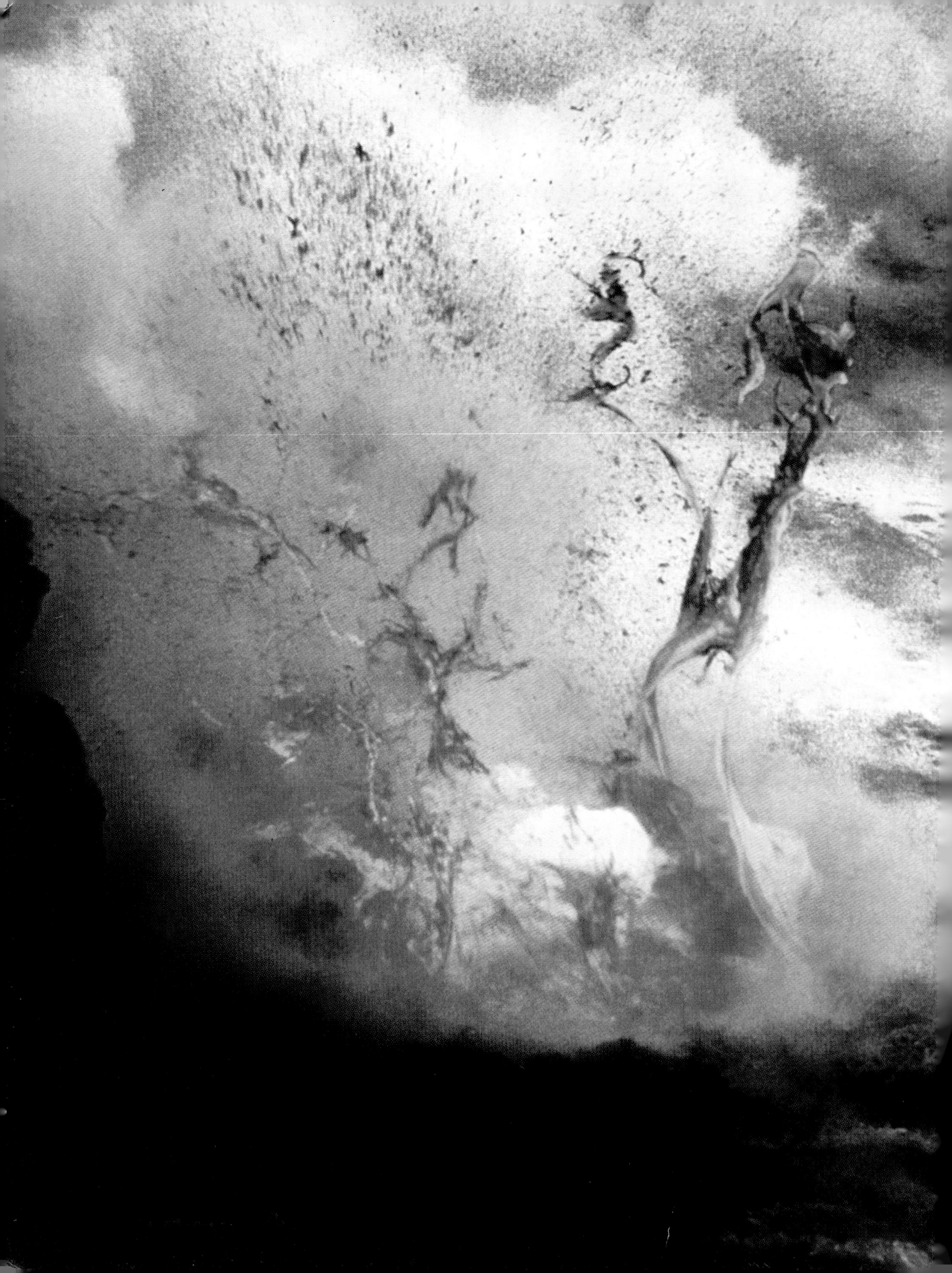

Reflecting

Back to the Beginning

You have been investigating Our Dynamic Planet in many ways. How have your ideas changed since the beginning of the investigation? Look at the following questions and write down your ideas in your journal:

- What are volcanoes and why do they occur where they do?
- What are earthquakes and what causes them?
- How are earthquakes and volcanoes related?
- How do mountains form?

How has your thinking about earthquakes, volcanoes, and mountains changed?

Thinking about the Earth System

At the end of each investigation, you thought about how your findings connected with the Earth system. Consider what you have learned about the Earth system. Refer to the *Earth System Connection* sheet that you have been building up throughout this module.

- What connections between Dynamic Planet and the Earth system have you been able to find?

Thinking about Scientific Inquiry

You have used inquiry processes throughout the module. Review the investigations you have done and the inquiry processes you have used.

- What scientific inquiry processes did you use?
- How did scientific inquiry processes help you learn about the Dynamic Planet?

A New Beginning!

Not so much an ending as a new beginning!

This investigation into *Our Dynamic Planet* is now completed. However, this is not the end of the story. You will see the importance of Earth's dynamic events where you live and everywhere you travel. Be alert for opportunities to observe the importance of *Our Dynamic Planet* and add to your understanding.

The Big Picture

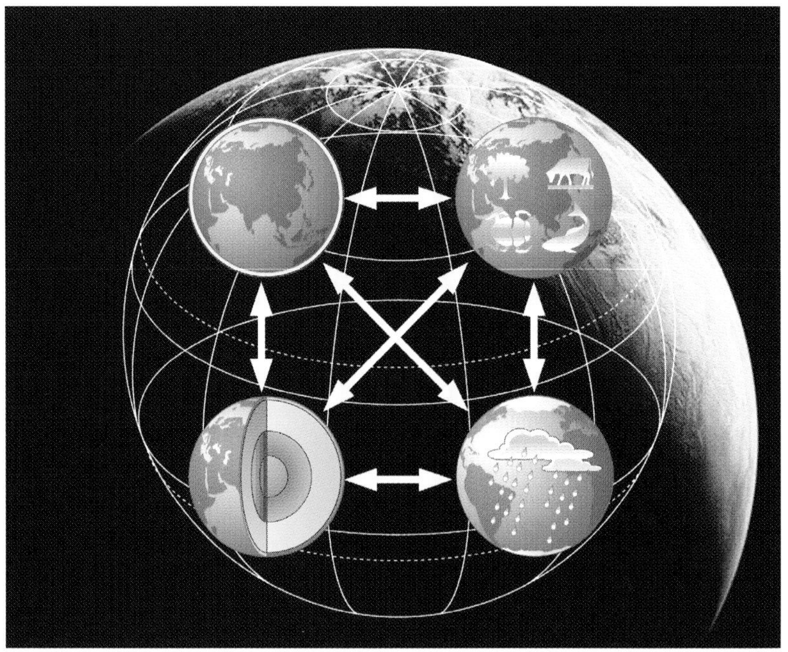

Key Concepts

Earth is a set of closely linked systems.

Earth's processes are powered by two sources: the Sun, and Earth's own inner heat.

The geology of Earth is dynamic, and has evolved over 4.5 billion years.

The geological evolution of Earth has left a record of its history that geoscientists interpret.

We depend upon Earth's resources—both mined and grown.

Glossary

Asthenosphere – A region of the Earth's interior immediately below the lithosphere where mantle rocks are hot enough and under enough pressure to deform, change shape and flow.

Biosphere – The part of the Earth System that includes all living organisms (animals and plants) and also dead and decaying plant matter.

Continent – One of the Earth's major landmasses.

Continental drift – A theory proposed by Alfred Wegener (1912) that proposed that the continents' positions on the globe are not fixed and that the continents have moved (and continue to move) about the globe during the course of geologic time.

Controlled test – A controlled test, or experiment, is one in which all other variables are held constant except for one. This procedure allows the experimenter to find out which variable in the test is giving a particular result.

Convection – The density-driven movement of a fluid material. Often, convection is driven by either heating from below or cooling from above the fluid.

Convection cell – A pattern of fluid movement where at one side material rises, moves laterally, then eventually sinks again to return back to its starting point.

Core – The central part of the Earth, beginning at a depth of about 2900 km, and consisting of iron-nickel alloy. It consists of a liquid outer core and solid inner core.

Cross section – A diagram showing features along a vertical plane.

Crust – The outermost layer of the Earth, composed of rock, representing less than 0.1% of the Earth's total volume.

Data – Observations, both quantitative and qualitative, from which conclusions can be inferred.

Density – Mass per unit volume.

Design – A plan for investigation. This could be a laboratory experiment, model, simulation, field study, or other type of investigation.

Earth System – A term used to describe the Earth as a set of closely interacting systems, including all subsystems, like the geosphere, lithosphere, atmosphere, hydrosphere, and biosphere.

Earthquake – A sudden motion or trembling in the Earth caused by the abrupt release of slowly accumulated strain.

Evidence – Data that support or contradict a scientific hypothesis or conclusion.

Experiment – A fair and objective test of a hypothesis.

Fault – A fracture or fracture zone along which there has been displacement of one mass of rock relative to another, parallel to the fracture.

Findings – Experimental results or conclusions.

Geoscientist – A person who is trained in and works in any of the geological sciences.

Geosphere – The part of the Earth System that includes the crust, mantle, and inner and outer core.

Glacier – A large and long-lasting mass of ice that is formed on land by compaction and recrystallization of snow, which flows downhill or outward under the force of its own weight.

Hydrosphere – The part of the Earth system that includes all the planet's water, including oceans, lakes, rivers, groundwater, ice, and water vapor.

Hypothesis – A statement that can be proved or disproved by experimental or observational evidence; a scientist's best estimation, based on scientific knowledge and assumptions, of the results of an experiment.

Ice sheet – A dome-shaped or sheet-like mass of glacier ice that covers a large area of a continent. The glacier ice of the ice sheet flows outward in all directions under its own weight.

Inquiry – Inquiry is the process of finding answers to questions through a variety of methods. These can include research, fair testing, using models, asking experts, or many other methods.

Inquiry processes – Inquiry processes are the methods used by scientists to find answers to questions. They include hypothesizing, observing, recording, analyzing, concluding, communicating, and others.

Inquiry questions – Inquiry questions are those questions designed to be answered through a systematic, scientific process.

Lithosphere – A term used in plate tectonics that refers to the rigid outer portion of the Earth. The lithosphere is composed of the crust and the uppermost portion of the mantle.

Lithospheric plates – A term used in plate tectonics that refers to the distinct and separate portions into which the lithosphere is subdivided.

Magma – Naturally occurring molten rock material, generated within the Earth from which igneous rocks are derived through solidification and related processes.

Mantle – The zone of the Earth beneath the crust and above the core. It is divided into the upper mantle and the lower mantle.

Melting – The process by which a solid material changes state to a liquid because of an increase in temperature.

Melting point – The temperature at which a solid material melts to a liquid.

Mid-oceanic ridge – A continuous median mountain ridge extending through an ocean, which is seismically active and often has a central rift valley and rugged topography. Mid-oceanic ridges are divergent plate boundaries and are the site of sea-floor spreading and the formation of new oceanic crust.

Mineral – An inorganic, naturally occurring solid material that has a definite chemical composition consisting of atoms and/or molecules that are arranged in a regular pattern.

Model – A model is a representation of a process, system, or object that is too big, too small, too unwieldy, or too unsafe to test directly.

Modeling – Modeling is the process by which a representation of a process, system, or object is used to investigate a scientific question.

Mountains – Any part of the Earth's crust higher than a hill, elevated at least 300 m (1000 feet) above the surrounding land.

Natural hazard – An event that arises from dynamic processes on Earth that can affect the lives, livelihood, and property of people (for example, earthquakes, volcanic eruptions, landslides, hurricanes).

Observations – Data collected using the senses.

Pangea – A supercontinent that existed 200 to 300 million years ago and included most of the continental crust of the Earth.

Plate – A segment of the Earth's lithosphere.

Plate boundary – A zone of seismic and tectonic activity along the edges of lithospheric (tectonic) plates.

Plate tectonics – The theory in which the lithosphere is divided into a number of plates, and the study of how the plates move and interact with one another.

Prediction – A prediction is a reasonable estimate of the outcome of a scientific test. Predictions are based upon prior knowledge, previous experimental results, and other research.

Pressure – Pressure is the force exerted across a surface divided by the surface area of that surface.

Record – To make a note of observations and events. Recording can be done on paper, electronically or through other means of communication such as video, sound recording, or photography.

Refraction – The deflection (or change in direction) of a ray of light or wave due to changes in its velocity as it passes from one medium to another.

Research report – A record of the processes and results of an investigation.

Results – Findings from an investigation.

Rock – A natural occuring solid material which is either a collection of one or more minerals, a body of mixed mineral matter, or solid organic matter.

Scientific inquiry – The process of investigating scientific questions in a systematic and reproducible manner.

Scientific processes – The methods used by scientists to investigate questions, record data, and analyze results.

Sediment – Particles of solid material that have been moved from their place of origin by wind, running water, or glacier ice and deposited on a surface.

Seismic wave – A general term for all elastic waves produced by earthquakes or artificially through explosions (Syn: earthquake wave).

Seismograph – An instrument that detects, magnifies, and records seismic waves.

Subduction zone – A long belt on the Earth where one plate dives down beneath another plate at some angle.

Supercontinent – A term for a large landmass formed by the collision and joining of several continental landmasses into a single, large continent.

Tectonic plates – Another term for lithospheric plates.

Theory – An explanation of why and how a specific natural phenomenon occurs that has been based on the support of considerable evidence and testing. Hypotheses that have been subjected to considerable testing and scrutiny, but have not been disproved, can evolve into theories. In turn, theories may be redefined as new hypotheses are tested.

Variables – The things about an experiment that can be changed by the researcher. In a fair test, only one variable at a time is changed.

Volcanic ash – Fine volcanic material (less than 2 mm in diameter) that can be ejected from a volcanic vent during an explosive eruption. Volcanic ash is the finest category of pyroclastic material (material ejected through the air during a volcanic eruption).

Volcano – A vent in the surface of the Earth through which magma and associated gases and ash erupt.

Wave – A motion that travels through a material and carries energy from one place to another.

The American Geological Institute and Investigating Earth Systems

Imagine more than 500,000 Earth scientists worldwide sharing a common voice, and you've just imagined the mission of the American Geological Institute. Our mission is to raise public awareness of the Earth sciences and the role that they play in mankind's use of natural resources, mitigation of natural hazards, and stewardship of the environment. For more than 50 years, AGI has served the scientists and teachers of its Member Societies and hundreds of associated colleges, universities, and corporations by producing Earth science educational materials, *Geotimes*–a geoscience news magazine, GeoRef–a reference database, and government affairs and public awareness programs.

So many important decisions made every day that affect our lives depend upon an understanding of how our Earth works. That's why AGI created *Investigating Earth Systems*. In your *Investigating Earth Systems* classroom, you'll discover the wonder and importance of Earth science. As you investigate minerals, soil, or oceans — do field work in nearby beaches, parks, or streams, explore how fossils form, understand where your energy resources come from, or find out how to forecast weather — you'll gain a better understanding of Earth science and its importance in your life.

We would like to thank the National Science Foundation and the AGI Foundation Members that have been supportive in bringing Earth science to students. The Chevron Corporation provided the initial leadership grant, with additional contributions from the following AGI Foundation Members: Anadarko Petroleum Corp., The Anschutz Foundation, Baker Hughes Foundation, Barrett Resources Corp., Elizabeth and Stephen Bechtel, Jr. Foundation, BPAmoco Foundation, Burlington Resources Foundation, CGG Americas, Inc., Conoco Inc., Consolidated Natural Gas Foundation, Diamond Offshore Co., Dominion Exploration & Production, Inc., EEX Corp., ExxonMobil Foundation, Global Marine Drilling Co., Halliburton Foundation, Inc., Kerr McGee Foundation, Maxus Energy Corp., Noble Drilling Corp., Occidental Petroleum Charitable Foundation, Parker Drilling Co., Phillips Petroleum Co., Santa Fe Snyder Corp., Schlumberger Foundation, Shell Oil Company Foundation, Southwestern Energy Co., Texaco, Inc., Texas Crude Energy, Inc., Unocal Corp. USX Foundation (Marathon Oil Co.).

We at AGI wish you success in your exploration of the Earth System!

Michael J. Smith
Director of Education, AGI

Marcus E. Milling
Executive Director, AGI